HABITAT

HABITAT

THE FIELD GUIDE TO DECORATING

LAUREN LIESS

PHOTOGRAPHY BY HELEN NORMAN

ABRAMS, NEW YORK

"Every work of man which has beauty in it must have some meaning also; that the presence of any beauty in a piece of handicraft implies that the mind of the man who made it was more or less excited at the time, was lifted somewhat above the commonplace; that he had something to communicate to his fellows which they did not know or feel before, and which they would never have known or felt if he had not been there to force them to it." —**WILLIAM MORRIS, 1841**

{ To my "Beautiful Grandmother," Patricia Cox, who has led me to that indescribable spark of excitement more times than I can count. Your encouragement to follow this dream of mine has meant more to me than you'll ever know. }

Editor **REBECCA KAPLAN**
Designer **SARAH GIFFORD**
Production Manager **DENISE LACONGO**

Library of Congress Control Number: 2014959572
ISBN: 978-1-4197-1785-7

Printed and bound in the United States
10 9 8 7 6 5 4 3 2

Abrams books are available at special discounts when purchased in quantity for premiums and promotions as well as fundraising or educational use. Special editions can also be created to specification. For details, contact specialsales@abramsbooks.com or the address below.

THE ART OF BOOKS SINCE 1949

115 West 18th Street
New York, NY 10011
www.abramsbooks.com

THANK YOUS

THERE ARE SO MANY PEOPLE without whom this book would never have happened. I'd like to thank the team at Abrams for believing in me and in this book, and especially my editor Rebecca Kaplan, for her insight and determination, and Zachary Knoll, for his kindness and attention to detail. Thank you also to Shawna Mullen and Andrea Danese for keeping the book on track. To Sarah Gifford, my book designer, who "got" me right away and created something more perfect than I ever thought possible. To my agent, Berta Treitl, who has championed me on and has truly been there for me in every step of this process, thank you.

To Helen Norman, whose photographs bring life to this book and who is not only an amazing photographer, but a kind and loyal friend.

I'd like to thank our clients—both those whose homes are in this book and those whom we've worked with throughout the years—for trusting us, welcoming us into your homes and lives, and most of all, for your friendship. I'm so grateful to you all.

I can't thank the team of people we work with on a regular basis to complete our projects enough. Paul and Nancy Johnson, your beautiful creations always exceed our expectations and you've taught me so much. To Michael Carr and the team at CarrMichael Construction, I can't thank you enough for never saying "no," and for your "anything's possible" attitude. To Preston and Brian Key and the delivery team at NRoute for your flexibility and senses of humor—yes, I see those texts! To Michael Franck, for your constant kindness and creativity. To Michael DiGuiseppe, for your flawless wallpaper installs, even when we've asked you to make tented ceilings and it seemed impossible. To the many wonderful suppliers, manufacturers, contractors, architects, and artists we work with—thank you for caring so much about your work and for making our clients so happy. Special thanks to Sid Cutts for one of the fastest and smoothest out-of-state renovations we've ever been a part of.

To my blog friends—especially Eddie Ross, Jaithan Kochar, Brooke and Steve Giannetti, Paloma Contreras, Joni Webb, Michele Ginnerty, Maria Killam, Debra Phillips, and Loi Thai—I'm so thankful for your friendship, inspiration, and encouragement; it means the world to me. To the magazine editors I've come to know and love, thank you for believing in me.

To my blog readers, you have done more for me than you'll ever know. You helped me gain my confidence and find a voice, and I am forever grateful to you.

To Meghan Short, my assistant designer, who is incredibly talented, kind, and honest, and makes me laugh on a daily basis. You're truly my right hand and you know you're family to us. To Febe, for all that you do. You are Wonder Woman.

Thank you to my friends and family for still loving me even though I've disappeared for months on end with work and the book. To my little sister, whose shoes are much bigger than mine though she doesn't yet know it. To my parents, especially, for supporting me unconditionally through every single move I've ever made. To my children—Christian, Justin, Luke, and Gisele—for being my everythings.

And finally, I'd like to thank my husband, David, who is also my business partner and my best friend. I get so much of the credit for this business, but you pour your heart and soul into it and work behind the scenes to make it all happen, often while sleep-deprived. Your tirelessness, thoughtfulness, wit, and love keep me going. I'm truly excited to wake up each and every day because of you.

CONTENTS

INTRODUCTION

{ **field guide** / fēld gīd – n.
an illustrated manual for identifying natural
objects, flora, or fauna in nature }

HOW TO USE THIS BOOK

Habitat: The Field Guide to Decorating can be read chronologically from front to back, or it can be used as a reference guide for specific topics. For easy reference, the index in the back of the book lists many of those topics and the page numbers on which they can be found. The book is broken down into three parts: the Fundamental Elements of Design, the Intangible Elements of Design, and a Room-by-Room Guide to the rooms of a house.

Opposite: My first field guide, opened to the page on the dandelion.

I STUMBLED ACROSS MY FIRST FIELD GUIDE, an herbal encyclopedia, when I was eleven years old. Captivated by its botanical drawings and entries about the herbs' origins and uses, I carried that thing around with me everywhere. I spent hours outdoors, hunting for specimens that looked like the black-and-white drawings in the pages, though I'm sure half of what I collected wasn't what I actually thought it was. I eventually got hold of more field guides, branching out into stones, edible plants, aromatherapy, and even mythical creatures.

As I got older, I began making my own field guides, filling notebooks with photos, sketches, and notes on all the things I discovered. I felt that once I'd classified something and listed it in a notebook, I had a better understanding of it and could, in turn, use that knowledge. I made remedies and homemade beauty products to sell at school with the information I'd gathered on herbs, plants, and oils, and I wrote stories based on the myths and folktales I'd read. If someone got a cut on the playground, I would excitedly begin tearing up little bits of wild plantain to place on the wound to heal it. Zits? Not a problem; I had just the tea to eliminate them. It was a weird hobby, but I absolutely loved it.

My fascination with nature has continued into adulthood and heavily influenced my work as a decorator. Nature always seems to find its way into my projects—in the artwork, materials, and accessories, or in the patterns of my textile collection. They wouldn't feel quite right without it. So when it came time to write a book that would compile a vast amount of material, I could think of no better format than a field guide (complete with definitions and pronunciation guide from Merriam-Webster's dictionary) to present my work and practical information in a beautiful, cohesive way, incorporating the natural edge that has come to define my style.

in the hereafter.
A mallet of cypress wood was once
...sed to discover thieves, but as far as is
...own, the exact procedure is lost.

...ODIL /*Narcissus spp.*)
...mes: Asphodel, Daffy-Down-Dilly,
...de Coucou, Goose Leek, Lent-
...rcissus, Porillon
...einine

...tility, Luck

...placed on the altar
...is carried for this

...om, the fresh
...d and worn
...hall surely

...num—
...ro-

...ifusa
...an Dami...

...ana is us...
...spells. It is also...

...(*Taraxacum of...
...ball, Canker...
...-a-Bed, Prie...
...wine Snout...

...er: ...asculine
...t: Jupiter
...: Hecate
...s: Divination,
...al Uses:
...To find out how
...he seeds off the
...ou will live as m...
...ds left on the head
...ell the time:
...d head. The...

...ound like c...wh...
...is infusion with p...
...s same tea, stea...
...bed, will call sp...
...To send a...
...w at the se...
...tion and vi...
...Dand...
...er of...

...loved one,
...r her di-
...asted and...make a tea.
...hic powers.
...aced beside

L...
F...

...Nam...
...nso...
...s Apple, Ghost Flower,
...ve-Will, Mad Apple,
...on, Stinkweed, Sor-

...the northwest
...brings favorable

...pp.) **POISON**

ON FINDING LOVE

They say you find love when you least expect it. Or, as I found out, when you stop looking so hard for it. This was the case with my family's current house. I found it online while perusing real estate listings "just for fun" one Saturday in the car on our way home from the beach. Real estate browsing is something my husband, David, and I have always done. We weren't *really* looking, I always told myself. But a listing popped up on the screen that I couldn't stop thinking about. I almost wished I hadn't seen it.

I read the description aloud to David, who was driving: "Breakfast room, living room with wood-burning stove. Wooden beams throughout, beautiful light. A two-car garage. One acre. Open house tomorrow."

I think I had him at two-car garage. Meanwhile, I was quietly freaking out. I loved our current town. I loved our house. We'd just finished renovating it and had it exactly the way we wanted it. We were finally settling in. We had a newborn, and David had recently quit his job to come work full-time for the design business. And this advertised house needed a *ton* of work. How could we move?

When we moved into it less than two months later, I officially declared us crazy.

We immediately began tearing the house apart. I designed our new house at night and on the weekends while keeping our clients' projects going during the day. We demo'd the kitchen and bathrooms, ripped out the floors, and tore down drywall. We cut huge holes into the side of the house for new windows, which we added wherever possible.

To escape the construction dust that pervaded every area of our lives, including our future lower-level master bedroom, David and I squeezed our bed into the tiny nursery upstairs. But the baby was boycotting sleep, which meant we didn't get much, either. As our oldest of three sons started kindergarten, true sleep-deprived, construction-zone, first-time-school-parents chaos set in: We did not have a clean uniform for our son when it was time to go out the door, we were missing forms, forgetting lunches and half-day pickups, eating dinners at the grocery store buffet, all while being surrounded by the constant sound of power tools. We were lucky it was a gorgeous autumn, which allowed us to eat meals outside on the deck, because the kitchen was long gone, and the only working sink was in the upstairs bathroom. Our office was in the unheated garage, so as the weather got colder, our only option was to dress more warmly.

Still, we were on cloud nine.

At night, while our three boys slept, and the house was finally quiet, David and I would sneak downstairs through the dark construction zone and imagine what our home would be like one day. We'd sit on the floor next to stacks of lumber in our soon-to-be bedroom, staring out at the tree in the rocky patch that would

Opposite: The walled oak grove of my cousin's mountain home is surrounded in a beautiful fog every morning.

eventually become our private garden and outdoor shower. To this day, the smell of freshly cut lumber makes me giddy. During these times, I would slow down to really see and appreciate each detail, and I remember the enormous amount of thought that went into every choice we made. Despite the chaos, it was exhilarating.

Yes, it was a dirty, dusty, inconvenient time, but we tried not to lose sight of the fact that we were incredibly fortunate to be redoing our home and creating something special for our family. It took us just under a year to "finish" our house, although I know we'll never truly be finished. When the construction ended and our vegetable garden was planted just steps away from the kitchen, this house felt different from any other place we'd lived. Life felt fuller and easier. Every single thing we've done to or brought into the house has a reason behind it, and it's so much more than I thought any home could ever be to me. I feel both relaxed and excited at home. Everywhere I look, I see a bit of nature, whether it's through one of the many windows we added or in a natural object we brought inside. Everything has its place, and our home is truly my refuge, my ideal "habitat." I live a different sort of lifestyle at a different sort of pace now than I did before this house. We made our house fit us, and, as a result, I feel at peace.

Did we find love?

I can say that I love my home as much as someone can love a thing, but what I think I really love is that it's the perfect backdrop for the people and the life I love. And *that* is its own kind of love.

Making my own "homeful" of decisions, along with helping my clients make theirs over the years, has taught me a lot about planning and decorating for people and their families. When I look back and realize how much one can truly affect the way he or she lives on a daily basis through the design of a home, I can't help but get excited. Decorating is about so much more than fabrics and furniture; it's about envisioning how people will wake up, perform daily routines, cook, eat, be with loved ones, party, relax, work, play . . . It's about *living*. The environment, or habitat, we create for ourselves should reflect every detail of our lives.

This book is a guide to what I've learned through my work and through my personal experiences, describing in precise detail how I progress step-by-step through the design process to make the decisions that ultimately lead to a fully realized vision. I hope it inspires you to have fun while decorating, to slow down, to enjoy the process, and to think carefully about how each decision and every little thing that you bring into your home will affect your life. If you're thoughtful and confident and hold fast to your vision, I know you'll find your own kind of love, too.

Opposite: My husband, David, found a set of antique apothecary pulls from an old pharmacy for our kitchen island. They're labeled with words such as *sundries, canary seed,* and *crocus,* which adds quirk to the kitchen and sparks conversation when we have company.

PART 1

THE FUNDAMENTAL ELEMENTS OF DESIGN

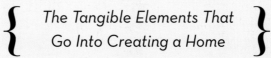

{ *The Tangible Elements That Go Into Creating a Home* }

CHAPTER 1

ARCHITECTURE

{ **ar·chi·tec·ture** / ˈär-kə-ˈtek-chər – n.
the art or science of designing and creating a building;
a method or style of building }

Opposite: The architecture in our clients' family room was so striking that little adornment was needed in the space. A mix of neutrals and simple sculptural pieces allow the space to breathe. We chose deep, soft upholstery and filled the room with kid- and dog-friendly materials for a functional space that feels sophisticated.

OFTEN THE BEST HOMES are the ones that feel as if they haven't been decorated at all. They are the houses in which the decorator's hand appears light or barely there. In order to design a home so that it doesn't feel overdone, it's important to understand the architecture, or the "bones" of the structure. When a house is full of structural flaws, often the only thing left to do—besides fix them, which can be expensive—is to try to hide them behind the decorating. But overcompensating for weak architecture almost always results in a forced, "overdecorated" look.

Before decorating any part of a home, first take a long, hard look at the architecture itself. Study it, noting its attributes and flaws. Does it have a particularly beautiful view? High or low ceilings? Interesting woodwork or lack of it? Be extremely critical. Can something be done at the outset of the project that will make the room more pleasing and interesting and eliminate the need to overdecorate or hide flaws later? Maybe it's as easy as adding moldings or bookshelves to a bland space, but it might be a bit more involved, requiring replacing flooring or windows, removing a wall, or adding a focal point, such as a fireplace or built-in shelving.

If you live in a home with little architectural character, consider adding some. Newly built homes often lack good woodwork, or any details at all, so making small changes, such as replacing standard baseboards with taller ones or adding interesting ceiling treatments, such as decorative plaster or beams, can instantly make them feel more permanent and timeless. Raising doorway heights or adding transoms above doorways will also make a home feel more spacious and give it room to "breathe."

Fixing flaws or replacing ho-hum details will have a massive impact on the overall look and feel of your finished home. If you don't like your living room fireplace, it doesn't matter how many pretty things you bring into the room or how well you decorate it; unless you fix or replace the fireplace, you'll never be completely satisfied with the space, because a fireplace is a major focal point in any room.

Opposite: The simple iron stair rail in our home came about from a collaboration with a local metal craftsman, Tom Owens. We widened the stairs, making them easier for tiny kid feet to navigate, by attaching pickets to the outside of the steps to allow the full width of each tread to be walked upon.

Above: In this living room, built-in bookshelves were added for architectural interest and are conveniently located near the fireplace, where my client likes to read nightly. We painted the window frames and doors black for a stark contrast against the white walls.

It's best to take the design process slowly if need be and build up each room in your home from a solid foundation of knowledge, which starts with the history of the place. Research the age and history of your home to determine what types of architectural elements are appropriate so that any changes you make look and feel authentic (see Chapter 14, on Authenticity). A Mediterranean-style house, for example, calls for very different architectural selections than a Colonial.

If your home is newer and doesn't quite fit into one architectural style or is a mash-up of styles, try to streamline whatever's going on inside the house. I have seen new homes that combine multiple styles—say, rustic beams with crown moldings, or two-story great rooms with pillars and Tuscan fireplaces; these interiors appear scattered and chaotic. The best solution is to pick one style and run with it, removing disparate elements wherever possible. If you feel that you're in over your head, consult with an architect whose work you respect.

Above: The painted built-ins in this farmhouse living room add architectural character and charm.

Above: In an extensive renovation, our clients' 1932 home was restored to its former glory. Rooms that had been previously chopped up over the years were rejoined, and new moldings and architectural details were installed throughout the home to reflect what it once may have looked like. The plaster ceiling details in the living room look original to the house. Architecture by Franck & Lohsen.

Above: In the plain-Jane dining room of our rustic contemporary 1970s house, we applied cedar planks to the ceiling for character and warmth. The room was instantly transformed, and we benefit from the side effect of the wonderful smell of the cedar.

Above: The stair hall in our clients' newly renovated home, though a pass-through, is one of my favorite areas in the house. When selecting woodwork for the space, we went with simple cove moldings and straight boards, which are slightly less ornate than what was once in the home, because my clients gravitate toward simplicity. Architecture by Cunningham | Quill Architects.

Above: Existing "straight" architecture in this mountain house dictated that we go with "straight" selections throughout: Straight, clean moldings, beams, and doors all add to the home's strong yet humble and rustic vibe. We also removed Tudoresque elements, such as ornate, "curvy" spindles on the stair rails and diamond-shaped window and door mullions.

Opposite: In our living room, we added the main focal point, the floor-to-ceiling fireplace. On the opposite wall sits the staircase, which balances out the fireplace (see photo of stairs on page 18).

I am not an architect, nor have I been classically trained, but as a decorator, I have my own, oversimplified way of thinking through certain architectural decisions. I've found that it's helpful to categorize architecture as generally "curvy" or "straight." Think about the house itself: How are the windows shaped? The doorways? The existing moldings and cabinetry? Are they ogeed (curved edge), beveled, arched, or squared off? If you're getting "curvy" answers, then this is generally the way you should proceed with the other architectural elements. Coordinate the fireplace mantel with the curve of the crown moldings, the cabinetry with the doors, the countertop edge with the woodwork, and so on. The same applies to scale. Higher ceilings and larger spaces typically call for proportional architectural detailing. Think about the architecture of the house as being grand or humble. Is it understated or bold? Everything is interrelated, and once you understand the general language of your home's architecture, decorating decisions come more easily.

Rooms are most striking when they have a strong focal point, or a point of emphasis where the eye is drawn when you enter the room. Common focal points are fireplaces, windows, televisions, beds, and even range hoods. Before delving into decorating a space, consider the focal point in the room. Is one already in place? If not, should one be? Can it be added or improved upon? In order for focal points to feel balanced in a space as a whole, consider the wall opposite the focal point: It's important that something called a secondary focal point provide a counterbalance on that wall so that the room doesn't feel lopsided.

Symmetry is pleasing to the eye, so look at or photograph each vertical plane (or wall) in a room, also called an "elevation," and scan it for balance. If it's asymmetrical, and you feel it would look better if it were balanced, as is usually the case, is there anything you can do to fix it? It might be as simple as placing a piece of art on one wall in order to balance out an odd window on the opposite wall, or it might be more effective to alter the "bones" of the room itself.

If something can be easily changed, then go for it. If it will incur too great an expense, or if you rent your home and changing the structure isn't an option, then there are ways to work around architectural flaws by masking them or diverting attention from them, which I'll discuss later in the book. In short, if you get the bones right, the decorating is much easier. It may seem like a daunting task, but with careful research and attention to detail, it's possible to create the perfect canvas on which to begin decorating.

Opposite: In the dining nook of our kitchen, there was originally only one off-center window on the left. To create a symmetrical elevation (see page 43), we added the window on the right. It was a simple change but allowed for a more balanced space.

CHAPTER 2

FINISHES & HARDWARE

{

fin·ish / fi′-nish – n.
1. the way in which the surface, as of furniture, is painted,
completed, varnished, smoothed, polished, etc.
2. the fine or decorative work required for a building or one of its parts
3. *Carpentry*- joiner work such as doors, stairs, panels, etc.

hard·ware / härd′-wer – n.
ware (as fittings, cutlery, tools, utensils, or parts of machines) made of metal

}

Opposite: A pair of shiny polished-nickel faucets contrasts with a chalky bluestone countertop in our family lake house bathroom.

FINISHES—ELEMENTS SUCH AS paint, wood, stone, metal, as well as those of the plumbing fixtures and hardware that are attached to the house itself—give our homes character. The "bones" of the home are its architecture, whereas the finish selections, often called the "jewelry," help set the tone and style of a home. Authentic, high-quality finishes create a sense of permanence and timelessness when they are appropriate in context with the architecture and style of the house, as well as the people who live there. Low-cost, shoddy, or trendy finishes can make a home feel outdated and cheap.

Touch is key, and quality finishes literally *feel* good. The *feeling* of a solid doorknob in the hand or a real wood floor beneath the feet is subtle but nonetheless affects our overall impression of a home. Wherever possible, select real wood, stone, and other materials over synthetic or imitation materials, and be wary of plastic products in your finishes.

Clients often ask about mixing or combining finishes, particularly in kitchens, where I have, for example, mixed stainless steel, polished nickel, brass, and iron. "Shouldn't they all match?" they ask. I love varying finishes, because in combination they can create depth and interest. When everything in a room matches, when all the wood is the same tone or when all the hardware is of the same metal, the room tends to look too contrived, too perfect, and it ends up feeling sterile.

Above: The combination of finishes on our clients' ILVE range illustrates how alternating finishes can be mixed for beautiful results.

Opposite: In my own home, a natural and vintage "vibe" was essential, so I collected vintage wooden doorknobs from Web sites such as eBay and Etsy. They arrived on my doorstep already beautifully timeworn. I combined the knobs with new, uncoated, polished-brass back plates that I sprayed with oven cleaner to advance the aging process. Against black Shaker doors, they make a statement.

That's not to say that if we throw several different finishes together in one room, they'll automatically look good. Combining finishes requires careful consideration, but with thought it's simple to select the right mix. The key lies in creating a relationship among the metal finishes and other elements in the room.

With metal finishes, I find it helps to think of them as "shiny" or "matte." Matte finishes tend to look more aged, casual, or rustic, whereas shiny finishes look new and more formal, so be sure to choose appropriately for the effect you're trying to achieve.

With wood, I often do a mix of different finishes with similar undertones, such as gray or orange, that blend well together. Not everything needs to match perfectly, but there should be a relationship between the different wood elements, and they should complement one another.

Opposite: In my kitchen, I've combined rusted-iron baker's racks set on the countertops with an unlacquered brass faucet, oversize rusted-bronze pulls on the cabinets, stainless-steel appliances, polished-nickel spotlights on the ceiling, antique blackened-copper cup pulls on the island, and a mix of bronze and brass on the pendants above the island. There is a *lot* going on here, finish-wise, but the finishes break down into three basic collections: black, silver, and brass. Each finish has a mate that it relates to somewhere else in the kitchen. The polished nickel ties in with the stainless-steel appliances, and the bronze and brass light fixtures tie in with the brass faucet and the black components.

Right: The built-in walnut cabinetry in this dining room has an oil finish that will patinate with age. The oak floors have been covered with polyurethane.

FINISHES

Timeless finishes, when they are in keeping with the architecture of a house and are made from materials that age gracefully, will look as good twenty years from now as they do today. Envision an old wood cutting board versus a plastic one or tile flooring compared to vinyl. Be careful with some of the trendier, newer finishes available in the marketplace. Think about colored wood finishes—from ebony to honey to limewash—and how hues are constantly shifting "in" and "out." The same is true of metal finishes, tile, countertops, and appliances. It's important to ask yourself why you're selecting a particular finish. If it's because you love it and think it's perfect for your home, and it just happens to be "in," then go for it, but if it's only because it's "in" and you're seeing it everywhere, be wary: That trend may end, but you'll be stuck with it. Trust in what feels right for your home and to your own taste, regardless of trends.

Below: Navy painted doors with black porcelain knobs and brass backplates make a style statement in a newly renovated home and relate to other elements in the house, such as the navy kitchen (page 49) and the blue-painted stair risers (page 21). Wallpapered sunflowers peek around the door.

Right: A classic polished-nickel rain showerhead in our family's lake house.

HABITAT

HARDWARE

Using antique or vintage hardware often adds character to a room or home. I especially like to use antique or vintage pieces with patina in new homes to add a sense of age, as if they've always been there. Antique and vintage options can cost more than new hardware, but it's possible to actually save money by using them. Our wooden doorknobs (see page 29) cost a little more than the typical doorknob from a hardware store but cost much less than new wood-and-brass doorknobs. I like to think of doors and their hardware as a microcosm of sorts for what's going on throughout the home. They should make sense with all the other finishes that will come into play, such as those of plumbing and lighting fixtures, of woodwork and furniture, and paint colors.

PLUMBING FIXTURES

Plumbing fixtures should feel substantial and solid and make sense with the architecture of the house. The plumbing fixtures throughout the home should have a relationship by either matching or blending nicely together. Be especially cautious about inexpensive plumbing fixtures that look great in photos but feel cheap in person. Typically, polished nickel and chrome feel solid, heavy, and "real" in person and are available at some great price points, but I've noticed that some of the less-expensive, oil-rubbed bronze, brass, and brushed-nickel finishes tend to look and feel fake, as they're often lighter, tinnier, and coated with a low-quality faux-metal finish. If you're set on one of these finishes, I'd recommend looking toward high-end manufacturers and checking out the fixtures in person before ordering. If you're looking for an authentic antique brass finish, be sure to order uncoated or unlacquered brass that will age properly rather than faux-aged brass, which doesn't look like the real thing at all. Many of the low-end polished-"brass" plumbing fixtures look and feel just like old builder's brass, which is very light and feels as if it has a plastic coating on it that can be scratched off over time, exposing the real metal underneath. If you want a quality, oil-rubbed bronze finish, try to see the fixture in person so you can make sure it feels solid and heavy. Don't be afraid to seek out antique and vintage sources for unique pieces.

FLOORS

Floors form one of the largest surface areas in the home, so the flooring material has a major impact on an overall space. We touch floors with every step, and they're quite literally the foundation upon which a room is built. Floors are often overlooked, and many homeowners assume that they have to live with what they have, but floors offer a great opportunity to inject style and personality into a home, so floor choice should be calculated. If changing out undesirable flooring is not an option, it's best to refinish, if possible, or try to hide it with large area rugs (see Chapter 6, on Rugs). With flooring selections, I prefer to keep a home cohesive with one main flooring throughout the entire house, and only bring in other types of flooring where it makes sense functionally, such as using stone in a foyer for easy care, cork for softness in a kitchen, tiles in a bathroom for protection from moisture, or carpet in a cold basement for warmth. Wood is a versatile overall flooring choice because it works for almost all types of interiors, is natural, can be very taste-specific due to the variety of options, and feels wonderful underfoot. However, in very hot climates it often makes sense to go with stone or concrete or tile as the main flooring selection. For an overview of flooring options, refer to the guide on page 39.

COUNTERTOPS & BACKSPLASHES

When it comes to countertops, I prefer to use natural stone because it brings a bit of nature indoors. My favorite stone countertops are soapstone, honed marble, bluestone, honed absolute black granite, and some white granites that look very much like marble; I'm generally partial to a "honed" finish on stone, which is matte (not shiny) and doesn't scratch as much as a polished finish. It also has a more natural look. Concrete is another attractive option that will acquire lots of nice patina over the years, though hiring a skilled worker is a must, as concrete is a tricky material to work with and install. When I'm seeking a countertop that looks clean and modern, I consider man-made ones such as Corian, Caesarstone, or Silestone. To make a natural stone countertop look thicker than it is, the best option is to miter the edge with another piece of stone to make it appear as thick as you want it to be. The edges of the stone are cut at an angle so there is only a small visible seam at the corner where they meet. I've created a guide for various countertops and their attributes on page 38.

Opposite: The timeless honed marble in our clients' kitchen will wear and change over time. It takes a certain type of person to appreciate the beauty in the aging process of marble and the imperfections that will develop with time. I believe every home needs a good dose of patina.

Above: The slate floors in our clients' sunroom are ideal for this transitional indoor-outdoor space.

Above: A classic white marble subway-tiled kitchen with brass and stainless-steel accents in a historic home.

Opposite: The tumbled-marble backsplash in this kitchen adds texture and earthy character to the new space.

As with most other finishes, the options for backsplashes are endless. The goal with a backsplash is both beauty and practicality. Ceramic, glass, porcelain, stone, and terra-cotta are all beautiful, but remember to make timeless selections that make sense within the context of your home (see page 31). Be careful of the many available trendy glass options, which can instantly date a room. Subway tiles are classic and can be very inexpensive, depending upon the manufacturer. Classic natural stone options, such as marble and limestone, tend to have staying power. Terra-cotta options feel warm and earthy and will last well in the appropriate setting.

COUNTERTOP OPTIONS

BLUESTONE

Bluestone is a general name for certain varieties in the sandstone family, and is dense, porous, and heat-resistant. It is available in a variety of beautiful grays and has a rustic appeal. I prefer it in a honed finish, which will give you a smooth matte surface. It should be sealed to prevent staining and resealed over time, as recommended. It can chip. REFERENCE PHOTOS: KITCHEN, PAGES 230–231; BATHROOM, PAGE 250

CONCRETE

Concrete countertops look warm, have a beautiful handmade appearance, patinate over time, and can be customized. They can be made in any color, so they're an ideal choice for those seeking a specific hue that isn't available in a stone or quartzite option. They need to be sealed to protect the porous concrete from staining, and hot items should not be placed on them, because they could damage the sealant. They tend to get small hairline cracks or chips, so those considering concrete need to embrace this aged look. Concrete countertops should be made and installed by a skilled artisan.

GRANITE

One of the densest natural stones, it resists chipping and scratching and is very heat-resistant. It's one of the best natural stone options for perfectionists or for those who do not want their countertops to show any aging or wear. Only a few timeless granite options exist, with my favorites being absolute black granite, the white granites that look similar to marble, Ebano, a solid brown granite, and certain slabs of Virginia Mist, which can look like soapstone, being solid black with a few thick white veins running through it. Be wary of most other granite slabs, which tend to have lots of veining, color, and movement, because they're extremely trendy and will date a home. I prefer a honed finish for a more natural look. A "leathered" finish is a nice option for a more natural look, but because it's not perfectly smooth, it doesn't make the best writing surface, so that's something to consider if you jot recipes or notes on your countertop. REFERENCE PHOTOS: KITCHEN, PAGE 222; KITCHEN, PAGE 229 (ON RIGHT)

LIMESTONE

Available in a variety of white-beige shades, limestone is one of the only natural stones available in sandy colors and is made from fossilized minerals and shells. Limestone is stunning. It's extremely porous, so it can stain, etch, and scratch easily, and it is much less expensive than many other stones because it's so widely available. A honed finish reduces the appearance of scratches and etching. Like marble, limestone is only for those who appreciate a countertop that will age and change over time. It should be sealed to reduce staining. It resists chipping and is heat-resistant.

MANUFACTURED COUNTERTOPS

Nonporous, scratch- and stain-resistant, manufactured countertops such as Corian can be a great option for those who want perfection. They are more modern looking because they are uniform in color and texture and can be made in thick slabs. Placing hot pots on them isn't recommended. REFERENCE PHOTOS: TABLE, PAGE 178; DESK, PAGE 253

QUARTZITE COUNTERTOPS

Nonporous and highly stain-, scratch-, and heat-resistant, some brands are also bacteria-resistant. Different brands, such as Silestone or Caesarstone, use different ratios of quartz to man-made materials, so research thoroughly to know exactly what it is you're considering. REFERENCE PHOTO: KITCHEN, PAGES 226–227

MARBLE

Marble is about as classic as a countertop can get, though it is not for those who want their countertop to always look new. Marble, a relatively soft stone, changes over time with daily wear and tear. Those who love it—as I do—appreciate the patina of used and aged marble. I prefer a honed finish, which ages beautifully over time and doesn't show scratches. Hot pots and pans should not be placed directly on it unless you're comfortable with potential discoloration. Polished marble will etch when it comes into contact with acidic substances, such as lemon

juice, and it can scratch easily, which is another reason I prefer a honed finish. Marble should be sealed to avoid staining. Red-wine spills can be an issue, as can water rings from glasses that have sat on it for a while. On our marble island, we have had red-wine rings from glasses left out all night, but once we cleaned them off with a damp rag, they eventually disappeared, first turning a little gray and then undetectable. The softer the marble, the more dramatically it will stain. We are not at all careful with our marble island, and we absolutely love it. REFERENCE PHOTOS: BATHROOM, PAGE 194; BATHROOM, PAGE 195; KITCHEN, PAGES 220–221; KITCHEN, PAGES 224–225; KITCHEN, PAGE 228; KITCHEN, PAGE 232; BATHROOM, PAGE 248

SOAPSTONE

Soapstone is soft, with antiseptic properties to resist bacteria, as well as heat-resistant and easy to maintain with mineral or beeswax oil, which act as a sealant. It's the only nonporous stone that does not need a chemical sealant. However, soapstone countertops can chip or dent easily around the edges. I have soapstone countertops in my kitchen at home, with the marble-topped island, and when I've accidentally banged a particularly heavy pan on the edge of one, it chipped slightly, but not enough to bother me. Part talc, soapstone is warmer than other, more dense stones such as granite. Soapstone has long been used as the countertop of choice for science labs because of the above mentioned properties. It's not as well known as other stones because it isn't as widely quarried or marketed. REFERENCE PHOTOS: KITCHEN, PAGES 228–229; KITCHEN, PAGES 234–235; KITCHEN, PAGE 226

A quick note about chopping on countertops: Don't do it. Even if your countertops can handle it, the blades of your knives won't stay sharp or last as long.

FLOORING OPTIONS

BRICK

Earthy and nostalgic, it's also slip-resistant and practical for high-traffic areas. Salvaged bricks are a beautiful, eco-friendly option. IDEAL APPLICATIONS: FOYERS, MUDROOMS, KITCHENS.

CARPET

Soft, warm, and often less expensive than other flooring options. Beware the adhesive being used in any carpet installation: Go for a no- or low-odor glue. IDEAL APPLICATIONS: BEDROOMS, BASEMENTS.

CONCRETE

Smooth, and the color possibilities are endless. Concrete floors patinate over time and can be customized in any color; they should be made and installed by a skilled artisan. IDEAL APPLICATIONS: MAIN LIVING AREAS IN REGIONS WITH A HOT CLIMATE.

CORK

Antibacterial and a renewable resource, cork is warm and softer than other materials. It's moisture-resistant. It's very forgiving when you drop glass or other breakables, and it is soft on the feet, so it works well in rooms where you plan to be standing a lot, such as the kitchen. IDEAL APPLICATIONS: KITCHEN, BASEMENT.

FLOATING HARDWOOD

It has the look and feel of hardwood but is not nailed down (the floor planks are interlocked together instead). The floating nature of the floor allows for expansion and contraction of the wood. IDEAL APPLICATIONS: FOR AREAS WHERE THE FLOORS CANNOT BE NAILED DOWN, SUCH AS ON A SLAB AND/OR IN A BASEMENT OR WHERE MOISTURE ISSUES COULD BE A PROBLEM.

HARDWOOD

Hardwood is one of the most universal flooring materials. It's easy to clean, smooth, and comfortable to walk on. It can be pre-finished or finished on site. My favorite on-site finishes are oil (WOCA oil is my first choice) and matte polyurethane. IDEAL APPLICATIONS: MAIN LIVING AREAS, BEDROOMS, KITCHENS, POWDER ROOMS, STAIRS.

TILE

Porcelain, ceramic, and terra-cotta are all beautiful options. Their styles vary greatly, and they stand up well to water. IDEAL APPLICATIONS: BATHROOMS, MUDROOMS.

STONE

Bluestone, limestone, slate, marble, to name a few. Stone is textural and beautiful and stands up well to water and almost any wear and tear. It can feel cold to bare feet, so, if possible, use radiant heating beneath stone floors. IDEAL APPLICATIONS: ENTRIES, MUDROOMS, BATHROOMS, AND MAIN LIVING SPACES IN HOT-CLIMATE AREAS.

Right: Glossy black hardwood floors up the level of formality in this historic home.

CHAPTER 3

FLOOR PLAN

{
floor plan / flôr plan – n.
scale drawing of the layout of rooms and
furnishings, etc., on each floor of a building
}

Opposite: Natural elements and relaxed linen rule in this family room that is arranged around the central TV and fireplace as the focal point. Collected objects are displayed on open shelving and layered in the center of the massive weathered coffee table.

A GOOD FLOOR PLAN IS THE KEY to a functional, comfortable room. The floor plan for a house is more than simply a diagram showing where everything will go; it's a guide for how the home will actually be lived in once it's been created. The elements in a floor plan will set up the patterns of life within a house.

The reality is that in a successful furniture arrangement, inches matter. A couple of inches too large, and a piece of furniture might not fit. A couple of inches too small, and it might look ridiculous. Taking the time to create a floor plan with furniture in place eliminates mistakes down the road.

I begin each and every project with a workable floor plan and subsequent to-do list, which becomes my guide throughout the design process. When I walk into an empty room for the first time, I don't always know how the furnishings should be arranged. I like to study a room first, thinking about who will be using the room and what functions will be required of it. Then I draw it out into a floor plan before deciding what type of furnishings will be needed.

Drawing a floor plan is simple. Our firm creates floor plans on a computer using a CAD program, but it's also easy to draw them on ¼" graph paper. Either way, start by sketching an outline of the room, making sure to include all windows, doors, vents, radiators, outlets, light switches, columns, steps, soffits, and any other permanent fixtures that are present. Note all measurements on your floor plan. Next, take a second sheet of ¼" graph paper and use each box to represent six inches—or use a CAD program—to draw the plan to scale, which allows you to get an actual feel for the size of furnishings that the space will allow. Once I have the general arrangements in a space drawn out, I make adjustments to the furniture setup until I arrive at the best one. Draw in traffic patterns in all rooms before sketching in furnishings so that you know where walkways are needed (see page 42); you do not want to place your theoretical furniture in the middle of traffic areas. Next, decide

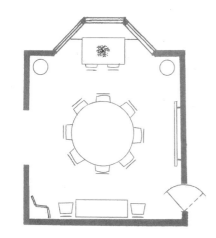

TIPS FOR FURNITURE PLACEMENT

+ Allow three feet of width for walkways in general spaces.

+ Kitchen walkways should be at least three and a half feet wide.

+ Allow at least three feet of space when entering a room before you reach a piece of furniture.

+ Coffee tables should be placed approximately 16–20 inches away from seating.

+ Build around focal points with conversation and walkways in mind.

+ Make sure that pieces are similarly scaled so that the proportions feel balanced.

+ To balance the walls, use art, focal points, and pieces of furniture so that walls opposite each other have relatively the same proportion of "stuff to wall."

Note: Keep furnishings at least six inches away from radiators.

what the main focus or focal point in the space is, and arrange the furniture around it so that it can be enjoyed by those in the room. If there isn't an architectural focal point such as a window or a fireplace, create one out of artwork or a large piece of furniture, such as a bookcase or an armoire. In living rooms and family rooms, it's tempting to arrange the seating so that it's the first thing you see upon entering the room, maybe set against a long wall, but it's best to have the seating *face* the focal point, not set up *as* the focal point.

In conjunction with the focal point, be sure to envision how the space will be used and what it will need for you to be comfortable in it. Make sure that walkways skirt around seating areas rather than go through them, as no one wants people traipsing through the middle of a conversation. The general rule of thumb is to allow a minimum walkway size of three feet between and around furnishings, but in tight spaces, smaller walkways might be necessary. Be sure that every seat in the room has a surface area for drinks, books, and the like within a convenient reaching distance. Include pieces for people to put their feet up, and think about where lighting will be needed (see Lighting, page 92). Make a note of the approximate rug size the room calls for (see Rugs, page 81). Play around with different furniture arrangements until you find one that feels right.

Focus on the room's main functions first, such as sitting by the fireplace, watching TV, or dining. The pieces in seating areas should be close enough that people can converse without shouting across the room, no more than seven to eight feet apart. Larger rooms usually require multiple seating areas for this purpose. Remember the lonely corners in large rooms, which are often forgotten. A corner can become an intimate little place of respite and quiet conversation during a busy cocktail party or a private, cozy spot for reading a book. Though not often the main purpose of a space, these secondary functions enhance a room and make it more versatile.

When determining what will be placed against the walls of a room, make sure that each wall is balanced with the wall across from it. For example, if there is an impressive architectural focal point such as a fireplace on one wall, something on the opposite wall, such as a piece of furniture or art, needs to be substantial enough that it can become the secondary focal point. The same goes for side walls: Make sure that when you are adding to one wall, the wall opposite is added to equally. This is simpler than it sounds. The easiest way to imagine this is to picture the typical arrangement of a bed on one wall and a dresser with art or a mirror above it on the wall opposite the bed.

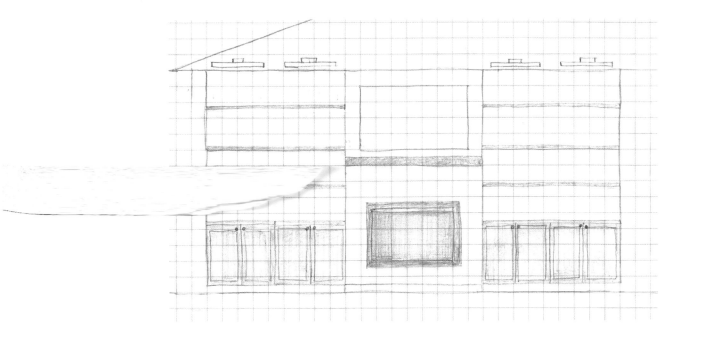

Opposite: A scaled floor plan.

Above: This is the elevation we used to plan the built-ins at the beginning of this chapter on page 41. To keep the architecture simple and clean, we installed the built-ins straight into the drywall without trim.

Once you've arrived at a floor plan that feels right, examine it for balance by making sure that furnishings are fairly evenly dispersed throughout the room. You don't want one side of the room to be more full of furniture than the other side, or it will upset the balance of the space. One of the best methods I've seen for checking balance is called the Balance Test, which I learned in the interior design program at the New York Institute of Art + Design. First, break the room down into four equal quadrants, and examine the furniture balance in each quadrant, making sure that each quadrant has a similar ratio of furnishings to empty space. If it looks as if one quadrant has more or fewer furnishings than the others, rearrange and add and/or remove furnishings until balance has been achieved.

ELEVATIONS

It's important to consider each of the four walls in a room. Sketch each wall, from floor to ceiling, drawing in all architectural details, such as moldings, windows, and doors. I'm not an artist, but I find drawing one-dimensional elevations relatively easy when I pay careful attention to scale and shape. This allows you to envision where you might want to add artwork, wall lighting, and furnishings, along with what style of window treatments will work best for the space. Draw each wall separately, and make sure that it's interesting to look at and feels balanced all by itself. When each wall looks pleasing on its own, compare it to its opposite wall and make sure they are balanced.

THE TO-DO LIST

Once I have a good working floor plan and elevations, I make a "to-do" (or to-purchase) list of everything in the floor plan and elevations, such as paint colors, sofas, rugs, curtains, and art, along with the things I may not have drawn in, such as accessories. I consider this master list one of the most important steps in my work, and it becomes my guide for the entire project. I always list furnishings in the same order, starting with upholstery and working my way down to tables, lighting, rugs, window treatments, art, and accessories. I provide a sample to-do list for every room in the house in Part III.

Once my floor plan, elevations, and to-do lists have been created, I begin looking for specific pieces of furniture to fill in my list. I check off anything that we already have, and as pieces are found, the floor plan is tweaked and items are filled in and checked off accordingly. I note the dimensions of each item for easy reference. I will often leave intentional "holes" in my list for antique, vintage, and one-of-a-kind items that aren't immediately available but that we'll be on the lookout for. I prefer to have almost every decision made—except for the "holes"—before making any purchases. If I or my clients fall in love with a piece with dimensions that differ from what is in the floor plan, it will affect the size of everything else, and I never want to limit my future decisions by having made a premature purchase.

As much as we all wish we had unlimited budgets to work with, the reality is that most of us do not. To keep track of the budget, I also include an estimated cost for each and every item in the room on the list so I can determine the total cost for the project in advance of purchasing anything.

Once a workable floor plan, elevations, and subsequent to-do list are created, the groundwork is laid for an organized project. Use it as a guide throughout the design process when delving into the more exciting selections, such as color, fabrics, and furnishings.

Opposite and above: A completed to-do list results in a fully realized space like our clients' sunroom. Doors open wide for a true indoor-outdoor space, and a TV on the wall facing the doors makes watching it from outside possible.

CHAPTER 4

COLOR

{
col·or / kə′-lər – n.
the sensation resulting from stimulation of the retina
of the eye by certain wavelengths of light
}

Opposite: Layers of blue in a bungalow dining room feel fresh and cheerful. Natural textures and such as seagrass, burlap, and wood keep it grounded.

PROBABLY NO OTHER ELEMENT IN A HOME affects its "mood" more than color. Color is often symbolic, based upon how certain colors make us feel and what mood they might stimulate in us. Blue symbolizes tranquility, because it tends to soothe, just as red symbolizes passion and stimulates energy. Much more than vibrations of light, color is the visual language of moods. It is used to evoke emotion and does so instantaneously. In nature, color announces each new season with its own palette: whites, tans, black, and gray in winter; chartreuse and yellow-greens in spring; deeper greens and fresh blues and yellows in summer; and reds, oranges, browns, and gold in autumn. When determining which colors to bring into your home, think about which emotions you want to trigger when you walk in (see Chapter 13, on Mood).

When looking for color-palette inspiration, the elementary question "What's your favorite color?" should most definitely be asked. Not everyone wants to live constantly with his or her favorite color, but it's a good place to begin a little color soul-searching. For example, my favorite color is green, but I haven't brought very much green into my home because the many large windows make it feel as if the green outside is actually inside. The views are what I love most about my home, and I like noticing the nuances of the changing palette of greens with the seasons. For me, bringing green in through fabrics or paint would compete with nature's greens, so I went with a neutral palette that allows the views to take center stage. Now whenever I bring in cuttings from the yard, their green stands out and makes everything else look prettier.

Look to things that you love to inspire your palette, whether it's a piece of clothing or jewelry, a painting, a flower, a page torn from a magazine, a rug, or a photograph. One of my most creative clients brought a few key pieces from her gorgeous handbag collection to our first "inspiration meeting" to share her style and the materials and colors she's drawn to. At a glance, I instantly got her love for vivid blues, sparkle, and polished metal.

Below is a chart of colors and the moods they most commonly elicit. Use it as a guideline rather than a manual, as even the pinkest of rooms can be made to look masculine.

To arrive at these moods in the home, the colors don't necessarily have to be on the walls. They can be brought in through the furnishings, fabrics, and accessories.

MOOD COLOR CHART

CHEERFUL	Ivory, white, yellow, spring green, fresh blues
AIRY	White, ivory, pale blue, pale aqua, light gray, pale taupe
CALMING	White, ivory, gray, colors with gray undertones, softer shades
ROMANTIC	Ivory, pastels, chalky colors, soft pink
BOLD	Saturated yellow, blue, green, red, black, white
DRAMATIC	Black, white, deep red, and other deep colors such as turquoise or emerald
MASCULINE	Navy, tan, olive, blue, dark green, gray
MOODY	Colors with gray undertones and depth, black
THOUGHTFUL	Yellow, ivory, white, colors with gray undertones and depth, blues

COLOR PALETTE

I like a color palette to be woven throughout multiple rooms, with the repetition of at least one color throughout, resulting in an overall palette for the entire home. This aids in creating a sense of "flow" and cohesion throughout the house. This repeating color can be a neutral or even a wood tone. When working on color palettes, I like to mix "fresh" colors with "dirty," murkier colors. "Dirty" colors have gray and brown undertones, whereas "fresh" colors are pure and clear. To me, the interplay between fresh and dirty colors is much more interesting than a room full of one or the other; a space filled with all fresh colors can lack depth, and one filled with all dirty colors is instantly enlivened by the addition of fresh colors.

SELECTING PAINT COLORS

Of all the design decisions I make with clients, paint color typically requires the most hand-holding. When a client's home is being painted, I brace myself for the phone to start ringing and the emails to fly in. If the color is ivory or white, paint-time jitters go something like, "It looks like builder's white!" or, "It looks so sterile!!" If the color is dark or intense, it's, "Will there be enough lighting in the room when we're done?" or, "Are you sure we should do this?" I almost always respond in the same way: "Hold fast to our original vision, and wait to see how it looks when everything else is in place." It's difficult to grasp the effect of a paint color in an empty room.

Above: A treasured turquoise vase from a friend sits atop a stack of books in shades of blue.

Opposite: Navy blue kitchen cabinets add a jolt of color to an otherwise neutral space. Navy plays throughout our clients' home in other unexpected places, such as on the doors and stair risers.

Clients are often surprised that the paint color is usually one of the last decisions we make in the design process. We typically have an idea of the approximate color early on, but the exact shade is usually selected *after* all the fabrics and finishes, unless we are letting the paint color drive the design.

I tend to stay away from overly bright colors on walls. I love bright color, but on a wall it can feel juvenile or cute. If you go for an intense color on the walls, it should be one with depth and sophistication.

DESIGN ELEMENT OR BACKGROUND?

After I've thought about a room's desired mood, I think about how much "work" is required of the walls. Should they be a major design element, or can they quietly recede into the background? To answer this question, I study the room and its bones. Is it architecturally pleasing? Do I want to play up the walls or downplay them? Are there interesting moldings that might benefit from contrast between the walls and trim? Are there odd angles that should be camouflaged using color? If there is no reason to call attention to the room's walls, I pick a good "wingman," or noncolor, that will recede into the background and make the other elements in the room look their best while giving off a nice glow. A wingman color is no less important in a room than an attention-grabbing color would be. The best way to pick a wingman color is to compare paint swatches to the fabrics and finishes you've chosen for the room. Choose the color that looks the most neutral when paired with these materials.

Opposite: In this living room, the fresh blue accents in the chair, the painting on the mantel, and the Chinese garden stool (lower right corner) wake up an otherwise deep and moody room with murky gray walls. The gold accents offer an eye-catching contrast to the gray and tans. Notice how much life the fresh green fern and the limelight hydrangeas on the mantel bring to the space. I believe that fresh plants or flowers are practically necessary components of a fully finished room (see Chapter 18, on Charm).

Below: A glass sliding door in our master bedroom opens to a private garden filled with lush greenery, including an evergreen clematis growing up one wall, and an outdoor shower. I kept the colors in the bedroom neutral to direct attention to the green outside.

I hear all the time, "I love color" or, "I want a colorful room," but a room can appear colorful without strong color on the walls. Instead of painting the walls blue, try to inject blue in other interesting ways, for example, with a blue sofa or accessories that you'll enjoy collecting over time.

UNDERTONES AND LIGHTING

A paint color varies according to the season and time of day and angle of the light. For example, in the spring, bright, newly green trees outside can give a greenish cast to ivory walls inside, while winter light gives those same ivory walls a grayish hue. Carry a paint swatch being considered around the room to see how the color changes in different areas at different hours.

Be mindful of your paint color's undertone. Every neutral has an undertone and can look like a different color when next to something else. The undertones to be most wary of are: pink, peach, yellow, purple, and green. Of course, at times you may want a certain undertone. For example, if your walls are gray and your rug is green, you might want to choose a gray paint with a slightly green undertone. To determine a color's undertone, compare it to something that is pure white, such as a piece of paper, and see what color it looks like in comparison. Practice makes it easier to spot an undertone.

Be careful when selecting light-colored paint or pastel colors, because the room could end up looking like a nursery. Choosing a light color that looks more like a gray on the paint swatch fixes this problem by giving the color a bit of depth, which makes a room feel more sophisticated. For example, if I need a light blue for cabinets, I select a light blue paint with a gray undertone. Once it goes up, it actually looks like a light blue but with a bit of depth.

PAINT SWATCH VERSUS WALL INTENSITY

Most colors look more intense on a wall than they do on a paint swatch. During one of my first painting experiences, in the bedroom of my post-college apartment, I wanted a medium-to-light aqua, but what I selected ended up being a very saturated robin's egg blue. Not realizing that paint looks much more intense when it's on the walls than it does on a paint swatch, I honestly thought the paint shop had mixed the wrong color. It took me a few more paint jobs to understand this effect. I find this to be especially true of yellows. Try to imagine the paint color on the paint swatch as a more intense version of itself once it goes up on the walls. If you are just beginning or are unsure, it's safest to do large test patches on your wall.

On the other hand, I've noticed that ivories, whites, and creams seem to de-intensify when on the wall. The eye sees these colors as white despite the fact

Previous spread, left: In this guest bedroom, we planned turquoise walls when we began the project, but we waited until all the fabrics had been chosen before selecting the exact shade of deep, rich turquoise.

Previous spread, right: The saturated pinky peach paint in our clients' dining room was quite a risk for them. They were unsure about the color until we installed the furnishings, but now they love it.

Opposite: Our client loves blue, but in her living room we decided to bring in the blue through accents such as lighting, pillows, and artwork, rather than on the walls.

Following spread: The browns and golds in the pattern of the chinoiserie wallpaper in this dining room are accentuated by the metallic grasscloth on the ceiling, which adds sparkle, texture, and depth.

that they're not actually pure white. Try to imagine the color on the paint swatch as a whiter version of itself once it goes up on the walls. If you are looking for an ivory or cream with a slight tint to it, be sure the tint is strong enough to be perceived.

Alternately, be especially careful with the undertones of whites, because what may look "white" to you initially can actually look like a color once it's up on the walls. Make sure to compare your white to a pure white so that you can be sure of its undertones.

WOODWORK

I often hear talk of making woodwork "pop," but that's not always what a room needs. Trim and woodwork should only stand out if they're worth calling attention to and if they are in keeping with the overall mood you're trying to achieve. If the moldings are particularly beautiful or interesting, or you want to highlight the classical architecture of a space, then it makes sense to call attention to the woodwork. If woodwork is unremarkable, there's no need to accentuate it. Contrasting trim adds a higher level of energy and visual interest to a space, whereas understated trim is more relaxing due to the lack of contrast.

Woodwork and trim are usually done in a semigloss or high gloss. A glossier finish takes the formality and "glam" factor up a notch. If I'm after a quieter vibe, I'll have the trim painted in the same color as the walls but in a semigloss finish. To create an aged and historical vibe, I'll do trim work slightly darker than the paint color or even in the same color but in a semigloss (see pages 135 and 150).

CEILINGS

If there is no crown molding, I prefer to wrap the wall color right onto the ceiling for a smooth and seamless effect. I like a wall color (or even wallpaper) to keep going until an architectural element stops it. If there is crown molding, then I change the ceiling color from the wall color, perhaps using a flat version of the semigloss trim, a lighter version of the wall color, a completely different color, or even wallpaper.

ACCENT WALLS

In general, I don't do accent walls, in which one wall is painted a different color than the rest of the walls, unless that wall is behind an open-back bookshelf. Accent walls can end up looking random and disjointed when there is no starting or stopping point other than the corner of a room.

CHAPTER 5

FURNITURE

fur·ni·ture / fər′-ni-chər – n.
the things, usually movable, in a room, apartment, etc.,
that equip it for living, such as chairs, sofas, tables, beds, etc.

Opposite: A mix of comfortable, nonpatterned furnishings allows the stone fireplace to take center stage in this family room.

AH, FURNITURE. PEOPLE HAVE VISCERAL REACTIONS to furniture that make my job interesting, to say the least. I have watched people get visibly distressed when asked to part with a ragged, saggy chair (because "it's so comfortable"), and I have seen grown men jump up from brand-new down-wrapped chairs in showrooms because they're "uncomfortable." I've learned to recognize the expression on someone's face when she's sitting in the right piece of furniture; there's a smile, yes, but there's also a sort of excitement in the eyes and a bit of "Is this really it?!" to the voice, or in some cases a confident, "This is it!" In my showroom, I've observed adamant shoppers' completely differing opinions on which pieces are comfortable, which are just the right height, which arms feel the best, and so on. There is no "winning" piece, because we're all unique, and we each have individual tastes.

When selecting specific pieces of furniture, comfort, function, and style are of the utmost importance no matter who is sitting in them. New clients often tell me they don't care what something looks like as long as it's comfortable and functional, but, fortunately, we live in a time where most good furniture is both comfortable and beautiful, and we don't have to sacrifice one for the other. There's never a need to buy something we don't like because it's "practical" or "comfortable," as there's simply too much available that meets all the criteria. "Comfort" is a relative term. We all have different thresholds for comfort, and, depending upon the functional needs for a certain piece of furniture, comfort itself can vary. For example, in a kitchen, it's not considered uncomfortable by most to sit on wooden chairs. Most people would balk, however, if it was suggested that their favorite reading chair by the fire be made entirely out of wood. It's not always this clear-cut, of course, so we need to visualize how we'll be using spaces and what functions will be required of certain pieces in our homes.

Opposite: A green velvet English arm sofa is one of the most comfortable and versatile pieces I own. It's moved with me and is just as at home in my now slightly more modern interiors as it was in our last, traditionally decorated home, left.

Above: The mid-height of the sofa contrasts with the high bamboo wing chairs. To bridge the height gap, we set a higher-than-normal side table with a lamp on it between the sofa and the chair so that the lamp rises slightly above the wing chair. This living room has a faster-than-average "pace" (see pages 62 and 86) because of the height variance and dramatic patterns.

In general, try to select furnishings that will endure the test of time, especially when it comes to the big-ticket items. Understand that trendy pieces will be "out" before you know it. There might be a case for adding an of-the-moment chair or fabric here or there, but make sure you truly love it so that you're not disappointed when it goes out of style. Steer clear of upholstered furniture with exaggerated proportions, instead looking for pieces with nice, clean, symmetrical lines. Small rolled arms are okay, but beware of large rolled arms and anything that could be construed as frumpy. Think of the classic tuxedo sofa that never goes out of style (see page 197), or the chesterfield (see page 200), or the English arm (see page 60) and the track arm (see page 198).

GUIDELINES FOR CHOOSING FURNITURE

When selecting furnishings for an entire room, be sure that there is variance in the height of the pieces. A room with everything at the same height tends to look monotonous and bland, and a room full of short and tall things that are, in essence, "roller-coastering" looks a bit chaotic. It's important to have a baseline height around which a portion—around 50 to 75 percent—of the furnishings lie, and, for the rest, vary the height slightly lower and slightly higher to create balance and interest. More height variance leads to more energy in a room, and less height variance leads to a slower "pace."

UPHOLSTERY

When it comes to upholstery, I recommend buying high-quality, even if you have little ones running around the house. I often hear people say that they plan to buy cheap upholstery for when the kids are young and switch to nicer upholstery when their children are older. I do not recommend following that route. Good upholstery can take a beating, whereas cheaply made upholstery cannot. Quality upholstery will still look good even after being pounced on for five years, whereas poorly made upholstery will fall apart as the pillows get lumpy. For the best upholstery, look to high-quality manufacturers who are using kiln-dried hardwood frames, which resist cracking. Depending upon the seat and cushion style, eight-way hand-tied spring systems are another indicator of good quality. Be aware of cushion content and the expected lifespan and maintenance factors of certain fills (down and down-wrapped cushions versus poly-filled cushions) over others. I love the relaxed look and feel of down and don't mind having to fluff a pillow, but not everyone would agree, so know how "hard" of a cushion you prefer, along with your threshold for fixing and fluffing.

The life expectancy for a piece of upholstery is three to fifteen years depending upon the quality of the piece, with an average of seven to ten years. This doesn't mean that after fifteen years you'll need to get rid of your sofa; you may simply want to reupholster it and have new cushions made. It's usually worth reupholstering high-quality upholstery, but it can cost more to reupholster inexpensive pieces than it does to replace them. Overall, if you buy quality pieces, you will save over a lifetime, because you will keep them longer. (It's also better for the environment!) My grandparents have had their sofa for over fifty years, and it looks great, in both condition and style, to this very day. When they bought it, it was the best they could reasonably afford. I've seen it in three different fabrics in my lifetime, and they've had the cushions redone a few times. (See page 170.)

Opposite: Laid-back, comfortable upholstery was a "must" for this busy family's great room. The sofa on the left is done in a washable linen slipcover, because it's where my clients' dog sits, and it needs to be washed frequently, and the other sofa is upholstered in an easy-to-care-for cotton-linen blend.

I love light colors on upholstery, especially white and oatmeal, so for worry-free maintenance, I like to use slipcovers. I prefer them perfectly fitted, or custom-made, so that they look as if they could be upholstery. I have four kids, a dog, and a bright-white slipcovered sofa in my living room (see page 23). I've had the sofa for a few years, and dirt and grime wash right out of it. And I don't like high-maintenance anything! The slipcover is made from an indestructible indoor-outdoor linen. Before throwing it into the washing machine on the cold, gentle cycle, I spot-treat any spills or grime with a stain remover, and it comes out looking like new. Twill and denim are other incredibly durable options for white slipcovers.

If possible, it is best to go to a store and see a piece of furniture and try it out before you buy it. Whenever you're not able to actually sit in a piece, pay close attention to the materials: the content of the cushions, what the upholstery is made of (see Fabric Guide, page 91), and the angle of the seat back of the piece you are considering. Then try sitting in pieces with similar seat depths at stores or showrooms to determine your preference, or measure your existing furnishings for comparison. Also consider how your existing furniture is working for you. Think about your likes and dislikes and quantify them if you can—a few inches too short, a few inches too deep, arm height a few inches too tall, and so on. Finally, always order a swatch of fabric before you purchase anything you haven't seen in person. For suggestions on the best upholstery fabrics, see the Fabric Guide on page 91.

SOFAS

The sofa often sets the tone for the rest of the space and can either make a statement or recede into the background. I prefer clean, classic lines that will work years down the road. Whether or not the sofa is upholstered in a patterned print or a solid depends upon the individual homeowner's style and preferences. For long periods of sitting and lounging, fully upholstered pieces (as opposed to part cushioned, part wood, or metal) are the most comfortable. Seat-depth preference is highly subjective and dependent upon a person's height and on the seat height, but for lounging and movie-watching, most people prefer deeper seat depths (twenty-four to thirty-six inches from the front edge of the seat to the back cushion), and for normal seated conversation, most prefer shallower seat depths (nineteen to twenty-three inches from the front edge of the seat to the back cushion). These dimensions vary depending upon the height of the sofa. Sofas with lower seat heights can be deeper, and sofas with higher seat heights need to be shallower so that feet can touch the ground. For those who might have trouble getting in and out of a sofa, such as elderly family members and friends, a taller seat height is preferred. In clients' homes where there is only one living area, we often select deeper upholstered

Right: My client's existing sofa in a neutral upholstery fabric had great lines, so we kept it and designed the room around it.

pieces with throw pillows that can be added or removed depending upon needs. If there's a TV in a room, I most often recommend going for a sofa with a deep seat for cuddling and one that's long enough to lie down at full length. I personally prefer ridiculously deep sofas.

I often hear people mention wanting a sofa with "comfortable arms" to lie down against, but in reality, most people lay their heads back upon a soft throw pillow against the arm, so harder or more structured arms shouldn't be ruled out.

It's important to think about whether tight-back or loose-back cushions are preferred. Tight-back pieces are streamlined and low-maintenance, while loose-back cushions are softer and need to be straightened periodically. See pages 60, 116, and 130 for tight-back cushions and pages 198, 199, and 203 for loose-back cushions.

Much debate occurs concerning the ideal number of seat cushions on a sofa. Three cushions are fine and more traditional, but I personally love a long, clean bench seat, and a two-cushion sofa looks a bit more streamlined than does a three-cushion sofa. (To date, I've never seen anyone get stuck in the "crack" in the center of the sofa. In fact, when I sit alone on my two-cushion sofa, I usually plop right down in the middle, on the dreaded "crack.")

CHAIRS

Just as with sofas, fully upholstered pieces are best for prolonged periods of sitting or lounging. They should be classic and comfortable.

WING CHAIRS Though often fairly upright, wing chairs surround you with their "wings" and are cozy and comfortable for intimate conversation and reading, especially with a nearby ottoman or footstool (see pages 20 and 163).

SLIPPER CHAIRS Though armless, slipper chairs are surprisingly comfortable and perfect for parties and socializing, because they're very open and nonconstrictive and can be sat in sideways (see page 124).

SWIVEL CHAIRS Best used in rooms where the chair's position will need to be changed frequently to meet different functions (such as watching TV or having a conversation). Be aware that small children love to spin in swivel chairs, so this might not always be the best choice (see pages 88 and 90).

ODD CHAIRS OR STATEMENT CHAIRS If space allows, I like to include a "statement" chair of some sort that doesn't have a partner as secondary seating. A statement chair should have real personality. These chairs are typically not used when only the immediate members of the household are present; they often see use during parties and events at which people won't be sitting for prolonged periods. As I mentioned earlier, not every seat needs to be comfortable enough to sit in for hours on end. Odd chairs are often not fully upholstered and can be made of wood, metal, acrylic, or other interesting materials. They're typically light enough that they can be moved from an underutilized area, such as a lonely corner of the living room, to a main area where everyone else is sitting when needed. I have a love for odd chairs akin to the love many women have for shoes and handbags. I can't resist a good, odd chair, and they can often be found quite inexpensively at flea markets or antique shops (see pages 67, 112, and 190).

Opposite: A quirky "odd chair" woven from willow branches serves as a surprisingly comfortable reading spot.

Opposite: Leather dining chairs in my cousin's vacation home in the mountains are both comfortable and forgiving. We added casters to the table so we can easily add leaves and pull it out to accommodate our large, boisterous family.

DINING CHAIRS

Dining chairs can be made entirely from a hard material, such as wood, metal, or plastic, upholstered on both the back and seat, or upholstered on the seat only. A fully upholstered dining chair is the most comfortable option for long, lingering dinners. I often use washable slipcovers on fully upholstered dining chairs in dining rooms that will see frequent use by children. In our dining room, we have washable slipcovers on our chairs, but we also keep a set of matching towels in the room to sling over our little boys' chairs during nightly meals, because I wouldn't want to deal with laundering the slipcovers multiple times a week.

BAR STOOLS/COUNTER STOOLS

Think about how frequently you will use bar or counter stools. If daily meals will be held at the counter, it's a good idea to select a stool with a back for comfort. If young children will be using the stools, a back also makes the seats a little safer. If people will not be sitting at the counter for long periods, then backless stools are a great option that can also save space in tight quarters. Bar stools will see a lot of wear and spills, so select cleanable materials.

COFFEE TABLES

The coffee table can be a major statement piece, and I sometimes select the coffee table first, even before the sofa, and let it guide the selection of the other pieces in a room. I like to use vintage coffee tables whenever possible, because they're unique and instantly add a shot of patina and character to a space. I also like to have custom coffee tables made, because often what I need for a space isn't available. Typical coffee tables are twelve to twenty-one inches high. Sixteen inches is my ideal coffee table height, and I try to keep it within a couple of inches up or down from that number. I like to place coffee tables approximately sixteen to twenty inches away from the seating so that one can comfortably walk between the pieces of furniture but can also easily reach the coffee table when sitting. In homes with young children, I typically select smaller coffee tables so more floor space remains available for playing and walking (often running!), whereas for my clients without young children, we choose larger coffee tables with more usable surface area. A large, square coffee table looks lovely when loaded with interesting objects, books, and flowers but might not be the most practical option when lots of play space is needed on the floor. When I need to go with something that doesn't take up much visual weight, I like to use a glass or Lucite piece. For families with children, I prefer a Lucite base with a tempered-glass top for safety and for freedom from worry about scratching the Lucite. (See page 23.)

TEA TABLES

Tea tables are slightly higher than coffee tables, at twenty-one to twenty-seven inches, and are often used in more formal living areas or those in which the family plans on eating meals in front of the TV. It's slightly easier to eat from tea-height. Most antique tables are tea height, because back in the day it was tea-height tables, not coffee-height tables, that people used. I've seen some beautiful dining and tea tables cut down to coffee table height for modern-day use, so keep an open mind if you find a table you love that's not sized quite right for your needs.

OTTOMAN AS COFFEE TABLE

Large upholstered ottomans can serve as coffee tables in more casual rooms where the primary purpose for a coffee table is putting feet up. They're also ideal for families with little ones, as they do not have hard edges.

Above: The large sunburst coffee table in this family room is one of my most memorable vintage finds. It instantly added personality and patina to my clients' newer home.

Opposite: In our loft, a massive hutch given to us by my father when we were married was built into our wall for a seamless look. We removed crown molding on the top of the piece so it would fit in with the simple, modern architecture of our home. The base of the TV is approximately forty-two inches from the ground, which is a little higher than usual, but when viewed from our sofa, which is all the way across the room, the height feels just right.

SIDE TABLES

Side tables are often afterthoughts, but well-chosen ones can help a room function beautifully. A basic sofa can be instantly transformed by the style of the side tables flanking it. One of my favorite types of side table for rooms where a bit of storage is needed for books or magazines is the tiered end table. Small chests also make good side tables. Think about the arm height of the seating where the side tables will be placed. I try to keep side tables within a couple of inches of arm height, so that they look proportionate with the seating. When side tables are too high for the piece they are next to, they tend to look unstable, especially when large lamps are placed on them. When I'm designing custom end tables, I make them just an inch or two below the arm height. Many side tables sold in stores hover around the twenty-eight- to thirty-inch height, which is often too high for the typical sofa and chair arms, which is twenty-three to twenty-four inches high, so be sure to know the measurements of a side table before you buy it, and understand how it will look in proportion to the piece of furniture it will be sitting next to. Side tables flanking a piece of furniture do not have to match, but they should be of a similar size and scale, and they should be within an inch or two of the same height. I often use mismatched side tables flanking a sofa for a "collected" look and top them with a pair of identical lamps for continuity. When the height of side tables is off, I like to use a stack of books to raise the lamp on the lower table to the same height as the lamp on the higher table.

CONSOLES AND SIDEBOARDS

Opposite: Old French market baskets store magazines, blankets, and other necessities in a console behind the sofa.

Consoles work both flush against walls and behind sofas with a pair of lamps on top. Parsons consoles, which are simple and stylish with straight, square legs, are particularly versatile, but when a client has storage needs, I prefer to use a piece with shelving, drawers, or doors to stow things away. When determining the size for a console behind a sofa, I like it to be at within an inch or two of the height of the sofa back.

MEDIA UNITS

I often use sideboards and cabinets to store electronic equipment, because they're more interesting to look at than the average media unit. TV height is a matter of personal preference, but, depending upon the seating's distance from the TV, I find that most people like for the bottom of the TV to be around thirty-six inches high or lower, so they don't have to strain their necks. Typically, the closer to a TV the seating is, the lower the TV should be.

DINING TABLES AND SIDEBOARDS

Dining tables can be made out of a variety of materials—wood, metal, laminate, stone, concrete, glass—so think about which material feels right to you and which works best within the greater context of your home. Try to choose the largest table possible for the space. The rule of thumb is that each seat takes up approximately two feet of tabletop space, so a seven-foot table can seat three people on each side and one on each end for a total of eight comfortable seats. At large gatherings, it would be possible to squeeze in additional seating, as long as everyone is okay with rubbing elbows. Typical tables are thirty-six to forty-four inches wide, though a much narrower, tavern-style table of around thirty inches or so can be quite cozy and intimate.

Opposite: This dining room was designed around my clients' existing burled dining table and Parsons chairs. We slipcovered the Parsons chairs to the floor in a charcoal linen for drama and added two new green-velvet host chairs for a jolt of color.

Left: In this dining room we had our client's old hutch painted white and applied grass cloth to the back of it, providing a nice contrast with her stained-wood table. A treasured silver julep-cup collection lines the shelves.

For custom dining tables, I typically do a width of somewhere around thirty-six to forty inches for a fairly close conversation distance. The style should be interesting enough that it looks as good on its own as it does when it's fully set with tableware and a centerpiece. Kitchen tables should be of a durable material, such as a wood with a finish that won't scratch or stain, whereas dining tables that are used less frequently can be of a more delicate nature.

Sideboards should have a strong relationship with the dining room table by either contrasting with it or blending with it. I often go the contrasting route, so if I'm using a stained-wood dining table, I'll select a painted sideboard, one with a different wood stain, or one made out of a different material altogether, such as metal, laminate, or stone.

DESKS

Traditional desks with drawers are practical for work and storage, small writing desks serve well for using a laptop, and a table with a large work surface is ideal for those who prefer to spread out their materials. The ideal height for a desk is between twenty-nine and thirty inches, depending on your own height and where your knees will fit when you are seated.

DESK CHAIRS

Depending upon your needs (such as wheels and ergonomics), you may opt for a traditional, swivel desk chair with wheels or possibly a dining chair. Comfortable dining chairs are my first choice when wheels aren't a requirement, because they offer more style options.

BEDS

Setting the tone for the entire space, the bed is generally the focal point of the bedroom. It's also the piece of furniture in which we spend the most time. Upholstered beds and headboards are ideal for those who read a lot in bed, but for those who like to read in bed but who have a wood or metal headboard, a set of Euro pillows behind standard pillows will provide sufficient comfort and support. Four-posters and canopies have a traditional, classic look, whereas beds with lower profiles are more modern in style.

NIGHTSTANDS AND DRESSERS

Opposite: In our master bedroom, an antique marble-topped table with a chair in front of it is used in lieu of a nightstand so that we have a small workstation when needed.

I often use small dressers as nightstands in the bedroom. King beds look particularly good flanked by dressers—as opposed to smaller-scale nightstands—because the huge bed doesn't dwarf the dressers the way it does nightstands. Writing tables are also a nice alternative to a nightstand in a bedroom where a small work space or writing surface is needed. The pieces flanking the bed do not have to match—in fact, I rarely use matching end tables beside a bed—but they should be of a similar size and scale, and the lamps on either side of the bed should be at the same height. If the tabletops aren't at the exact same height, you can use a stack of books to raise the shorter lamp to the taller lamp's height.

CHAPTER 6

RUGS

{
rug / rug – n.
a piece of thick, often napped fabric, woven strips of rag, an animal skin, etc.,
used as a floor covering; usually distinguished from carpet in being a single piece
of definite shape, not intended to cover the entire floor
}

Opposite: A blue-striped hemp kilim provides color and patina in an otherwise neutral, new sitting room.

RUGS ARE OFTEN WORKS OF ART in and of themselves. I could (and do!) sift through rugs at carpet showrooms for hours, just taking in all the details, patterns, and colors. Much like art, each rug tells a story and can make or break a room. Rugs add softness and warmth to a space, but each one also brings a different sensibility and its own special vibe. Because they generally cover such a large area, they can make a logical starting point for many rooms. I generally prefer rugs to wall-to-wall carpeting because they can be taken up for cleaning and they provide interest, though wall-to-wall carpeting is often a practical solution for basements.

So many different types of rugs are available to choose from that the possibilities can seem endless. I usually begin my rug search by thinking about function and budget and whether or not I want the rug to recede into the background or make a statement. If it's to recede into the background, I'll look for a natural-fiber rug or one in softer colors and neutrals with a tone-on-tone or a barely-there pattern that fits right in with the rest of the room's palette. If the rug should stand out, I look for one with a pronounced pattern, high-contrast tones, or intense colors.

I have a thing for antique and vintage rugs. They add patina and uniqueness, bring an interesting sense of history into a home, and can be incredibly soft. They're also practical, because many are made from easy-to-maintain wool, and the effects of wear and tear aren't as visible in them as in newer rugs, because they're already worn. But they can be costly, and it might be difficult to find selections in the necessary colors, style, and size at the right price point. Fortunately, many manufacturers and retailers now make new rugs that look like older ones at more affordable price points. I especially love vegetable-dyed wool, because it conveys the soft, natural look of antique rugs.

A variety of good rugs is available at almost every price point, and once I know my budget, I begin sifting through hundreds of rugs in that price range. Be careful about ordering rugs online. I buy a lot of rugs online, and

Above: An easy-to-maintain wool rug is layered over a sisal rug in this family room.

Page 83: The family-room loft at our cousin's mountain house is one of the kids' favorite spots: The mountain views are stunning, and the kids love looking at the antique, forty-eight-star flag and playing on the plush shag rug.

some do arrive exactly as pictured, but others look very different from their photographs and have to be returned. I've come to learn that some companies' photos of rugs on their Web sites look very accurate, whereas others do not. However, most major retailers' rug photography is fairly accurate, and smaller companies are often willing to take and send additional pictures if requested.

CHOOSING THE RIGHT RUG

In order for a rug to last, it needs to be able to stand up to the expected level of traffic for a given space. Use darker rugs or heavily patterned ones for high-traffic areas such as the foyer or under everyday dining tables, and save lighter-colored rugs made from delicate materials for rooms with less foot traffic, such as bedrooms. The chart on the following pages describes a variety of rugs and their most practical applications.

The ideal-size rug lies approximately three to twenty inches away from the walls of the room, with smaller rooms needing smaller perimeters and larger rooms needing larger perimeters. In a living area, furniture should, for the most part, fit completely on the rug. The back legs of a piece of furniture can be off the rug if absolutely necessary, but the front legs must remain on the rug or it looks too small. For a dining room rug, be sure to allow a minimum of two feet out from the edge of the table so that chairs can be pulled out without falling off the rug, though three feet is ideal. Cowhide rugs are the exception, and it's expected that furniture will hang off them.

Using undersize rugs is one of the most common decorating mistakes I see in homes. Many rooms are so large that standard-size area rugs are too small, so I often have a large custom, natural-fiber area rug made and then layer a smaller, softer-patterned rug on top of it for interest. Even if a room's size isn't an issue, I like the relaxed, warm look of layered rugs. The layering can also make for a softer floor space. You can layer thin or thick rugs.

Properly maintained rugs can last more than a lifetime and be passed down through generations. Rug pads should be used beneath rugs for the protection of both the flooring and the rug. Vacuum rugs regularly—say, once a week—raising the beater bar for delicate rugs and rugs with high piles, and have them professionally cleaned at least every two years. Clean up accidents and spills immediately, using proper care instructions for each particular rug, calling a professional if necessary.

When I come across the right rug for a room, I instantly know it. Although I mentioned that rugs are a great starting point for a room, I rarely start out with the rug. Because I'm such a fabric fiend, I typically let the upholstery and window fabrics guide my design. I usually have a general idea of the type of rug I'm looking for when I'm working on the fabrics and overall palette for a room, but, as with a paint color, I don't know the exact rug until I see it. When I do find the right one, I quickly form an attachment to it, because the rug is what makes everything else in the room sing.

RUG OPTIONS

TYPE	STYLE FACTOR	THE DETAILS	MAINTENANCE
COTTON	Cotton rugs feel charming and fresh. They often come in bright colors and a wide variety of patterns. I love a good striped cotton rug. **PAGE 112**	Cotton rugs tend to be flat weaves, so they aren't very plush, but they are comfortable enough to sit on.	Cotton will show dirt, and it stains easily, so it's best for bedrooms and areas with less traffic. Many cotton rugs can be thrown into the wash, so if the size is small enough, a cotton rug can be placed in a higher-traffic area and be washed frequently.
HIDE	Hide rugs feel chic and relaxed. They look great on their own or layered over natural-fiber rugs. **PAGES 24, 93**	The natural lanolin present in a hide protects it from dirt and spills. I use them frequently under dining tables for families, because the kids can spill away without worrying about stains.	Little to none. Wipe up spills with a damp rag.
INDOOR-OUTDOOR	For interior purposes, an indoor-outdoor rug typically looks a bit better from afar and, though not the softest option, is incredibly practical. **PAGES 166, 263**	Very kid- and pet-friendly, indoor-outdoor rugs are available in both natural-looking and bright colors and a variety of patterns.	Worry-free. Vacuum regularly, and take outside to hose off if necessary.
JUTE	I adore jute. It's so chunky and warm-looking, and it instantly adds texture to a room. It's available in different weaves, my favorite being braided jute with jute banding. I particularly like jute in a living room or family room because of how soft and textural it is, and it looks beautiful with other rugs layered over it. **PAGES 87, 88, 147, 148**	The fibers of a jute rug can stick to clothing like lint when people lie down on it. A fine fiber dust can gather underneath some jute rugs. Some nice jute blends are available, too, but they all perform a bit differently from one another.	It can stain fairly easily, so be sure to get spills up right away. Be careful of pet claws, because the fibers can pull up. Gentle vacuuming with the beater bar raised is recommended weekly to lift dirt from the fibers. I wouldn't recommend jute for high-traffic areas such as a foyer or hallway.
SEAGRASS	Seagrass is natural, textural, and comes in a variety of weaves. I love using it with other rugs layered on top of it for softness, and it's probably the rug type I use most frequently. It has a wonderful "hay" smell when first installed. Its color changes over time, starting out with a slight green tinge when it's fresh and eventually turning more tan. If you are layering rugs on top of the seagrass, the area beneath the top rug might stay green longer because the moisture is being protected there, so keep that in mind if you plan on moving rugs around seasonally. For banding around the edge, I prefer a color that blends with the seagrass. **PAGES 71, 131**	Seagrass is not soft and takes some getting used to. My kids have grown up crawling around on it and are used to it, but it's not the typical soft rug, so for play areas or areas where people will be spending lots of time on the floor, it's best to layer another, softer rug over it. Seagrass is available with or without an attached rug pad and is typically latex-backed whichever way it comes. It can be installed wall-to-wall and is an inexpensive alternative to many hard flooring materials. The seams are not visible. Be sure to use an experienced installer who will seal down the seams and all edges.	Easy! It's recommended that you vacuum seagrass once a week, and you can even sweep these rugs clean. Since the grass naturally grows near the water, it resists stains and water marks, but it's still best to clean up any spills immediately and dry them with a fan or towel. Seagrass is a fairly hard surface, so substances such as outdoor dirt can be wiped up or vacuumed.
SILK	Silk adds a beautiful sheen that makes a room feel more glamorous.	Typical silks are blended with wool for easier, though not carefree, maintenance. Silk rugs are best reserved for rooms with low foot-traffic or where shoes will be removed, as they are more delicate than other rugs. They tend to be costly.	Professional cleaning is recommended for spills such as water, and most cleaning agents can damage it.

SISAL

Sisal is a beautiful, natural-fiber rug option. It is slightly more refined than jute and seagrass and is available in a variety of interesting weaves. For banding, I prefer a color that blends with the natural color of the rug. **PAGES 116, 130, 153**

Sisal has a rough, frayed, ropelike texture. It's not ideal for baby and kid knees or for lounging on, but it is ideal for rooms in which you won't be spending a lot of time on the floor or for layering underneath a softer rug. It is also beautiful installed wall-to-wall in a living room or bedroom.

The maintenance is a bit higher for sisal than seagrass. Water can stain it although doesn't always; it depends upon the rug. It can discolor easily when exposed to chemicals and pet accidents. Be sure to wipe up spills immediately, and call a specialist if needed.

SYNTHETIC

Synthetic rugs can be practical solutions in areas such as basements or children's rooms, where budget and low maintenance are paramount. **PAGE 166**

Synthetic rugs are extremely child- and pet-friendly. They work well in high-traffic areas, though lighter colors will show more dirt than darker colors.

Synthetics clean up amazingly well, and they can handle some serious spills.

WOOL

Wool rugs are available in a wide variety of styles and colors, and they're one of the best all-around rug choices. Many antique and vintage wool rugs are considered highly desirable, such as kilims and Persian rugs. Wool is my preferred material of choice for wall-to-wall carpeting when softness is desired. **PAGES 62, 83, 140**

Wool is soft and comfortable to sit on and comes in a variety of thicknesses and colors. From flat weaves, which aren't plush at all, to dense, thick piles and shags, wool is incredibly versatile. Price points vary with quality levels and manufacturing techniques such as machine-made, handwoven, and hand knotted.

Care consists of regular vacuuming. Spills clean up easily from wool, and a good wool rug can last a lifetime or more. Ideal for high-traffic areas. Shag rugs have a special maintenance consideration and will shed like crazy for the first year or so and need to be vacuumed at least once a week to pull up excess fibers.

CHAPTER 7

FABRIC & PATTERN

fab·ric / fab'-rik – n.
a material made from fibers or threads by weaving, knitting, felting, etc.,
as any cloth, felt, lace, or the like

pat·tern / pa'-tərn – n.
an arrangement of forms; disposition of parts or elements

FABRIC HAS LONG BEEN AN OBSESSION of mine. I adore both woven and printed fabrics and buy small bits of vintage yardage for pillows whenever I come across a textile (usually online) I love. I can't say no to a fabric that intrigues me. I gravitate toward natural fabrics, such as linens, hemps, and silks. I have my own textile collection, and although drawing is truly difficult for me, I love fabrics so much that I felt I had to try my hand at them. I'm always storing up ideas for new designs, mostly based on plants, flowers, and other bits of nature that are meaningful to me.

Fabrics add layers of texture to a room, and their feel is just as important as their style. Fabrics, especially patterns, tell a story. They can be serious or playful, relaxed or formal. A few patterned pillows can change the vibe of a room entirely. Pattern preferences are completely subjective, and I find that people often have very strong opinions about them. Patterns go in and out of style, but I believe there's a time and a place for almost every type of pattern.

I often begin to design a room with a single swatch of fabric. It may be a pattern or a solid, but my goal is to select a fabric that is utterly and completely "my client." From there, I pull other fabrics, both patterns and solids, that work well with it into one big, beautiful, messy pile on my worktable. Initially, I pull many more fabrics than I would ever put into one room, and as I work through the design process and begin selecting individual pieces of furniture, curtains, rugs, and pillows, I choose fabrics from the big pile and move them into a smaller pile, which becomes the final palette to be presented to our clients. Spreading out the final fabrics side by side and seeing them together can be revelatory: This is the first real snapshot of what the finished space will look and feel like.

Often, I like to include something that's a little bit "off." Once I have all the fabrics that are right for the basic tone, I might add in a fabric (or two) that

Opposite: A pile of fabrics from my collection, Lauren Liess Textiles.

is slightly deeper or surprising, that stands out. It's tempting to go with a perfectly matching palette, but that can end up looking bland or one-dimensional (see Chapter 18, on Charm).

Everyone has his or her own personal preference for how much pattern he or she likes in a room. I call this the pattern-to-solid ratio. This is directly related to how "busy" a room is or how fast or slow of a "pace" it has. Some of my clients prefer that a room have a mix of patterns, and other clients like little to no pattern at all.

The more pattern there is in a room, the higher the pattern-to-solid-ratio. With more pattern, there will be more energy in the room, and it will feel busier. The fewer patterns and the more solids there are, the lower the pattern-to-solid ratio. The more solids there are, the more relaxed and calm the room will feel. Color also comes into play, because a mix of colors leads to higher energy, whereas a monochromatic color scheme leads to less excitement and energy. Neither is good or bad, simply a matter of personal preference.

Above, left: To add a little bit of "off" to this primarily peach-and-blue dining room, I brought in a pea green velvet on the window seat, which makes the color scheme more interesting and complex. Pea green isn't exactly a color most people would say they love (though I do!), and when I presented it to my client, it worried her. She went along with it because she trusted me, and she loves it now that it's in place.

Above, right: To determine the pattern-to-solid ratio in this room, add up the number of patterns and solids in the main pieces and make a comparison. There are four patterns: on the ottoman, curtains, paintings, and throw blanket; and six solids: on the walls, ceilings, chairs, sofa, rug, and pillow. So we have a pattern-to-solid ratio of 4 to 6, or a 2:3 ratio, which equals 66.6 percent. This is what I consider a medium ratio.

To figure out your preferred pattern-to-solid ratio, study photos of rooms you absolutely love, and pay attention to what's been done in those rooms. If the sofas and chairs are typically solid-colored in the rooms you love, and the curtains are patterned and the pillows are a mix of solids and patterns, you can create a similar breakdown in your own home. You'll notice right away whether you're drawn to rooms with more solids or patterns or those with an equal balance, and the more you study, the easier this quotient becomes to recognize.

I appreciate different types of spaces and fall in love with rooms of both high and low energy levels, such as a perfectly cluttered English country manor house or a dramatically sparse Belgian room, but in my own personal spaces, I prefer a low ratio of patterns to solids. You might notice that much of my work tends to have a balanced amount of pattern to solids, with few spaces that would be considered high on the patterned end of the spectrum. I like a bit of breathing room in my spaces, and that has become a characteristic of my aesthetic (see Chapter 11, on Aesthetic).

Above: This sunroom is almost devoid of pattern, so that the focus would be on the views outdoors. To add interest, we included a variety of materials, such as stone, jute, wood, linen, and velvet, and relied heavily on formal symmetry.

Opposite: This dining room is mostly solid with patterned curtains in my "Live Paisley" fabric. The feeling is light, airy, and breezy.

When considering pattern, keep in mind the walls, ceiling, artwork, and rugs. Rugs and wallpapers are usually on the radar when mixing patterns, but artwork and other elements are often overlooked. Other elements that can read as a pattern are light fixtures, intricate chair backs, and certain large accessories. Sometimes it's more than the subject of the artwork itself that creates pattern and "movement"; the grouping of the artworks and their frames can create a pattern on the wall (see Chapter 10, on Art and Accessories).

Many people's pattern-to-solid ratio preferences change in different rooms of the house. Bedrooms, for example, often have less pattern than other rooms, because a bedroom is generally thought of as a calming space where we go to relax and sleep. Once you've determined what your personal pattern-to-solid ratio preference is in the various rooms of your home, dig in and begin selecting fabrics.

Some examples of rooms in this book with more energy and higher pattern-to-solid ratios, pages: 61, 148, 152, and 200.

Examples of rooms with a calmer vibe and low pattern-to-solid ratios, pages: 135, 157, and 163.

Right: This Peter Dunham print boasted a beautiful border, so we had it sewn along the bottom hem of the chair and around the edges of the boxed seat cushion.

Pattern on large-scale elements in a room, such as curtains or sofas, has the most effect on the room's "energy level." If you prefer rooms with pattern but don't want a busy look, put patterns of different scales together. Multiple large patterns will compete with one another, but combining large, medium, and small patterns allows them to work together.

Combine different types of patterns to keep things interesting. A floral, a stripe, and a graphic pattern, for example, can work together beautifully, whereas three florals might feel like "flower-power" overkill, or three graphic patterns or stripes might feel a bit intense and repetitive. The recipe for many rooms with medium pattern-to-solid ratios is a generally textural-feeling room with solid upholstery or curtains laced through with a little bit of pattern in the rugs, pillows, and art.

If your preference is for less pattern or color, you can still keep your rooms interesting by varying their textures and fabrics. Mix velvets with leather and linen, and even mix like fabrics, such as linen, by varying the size of the weave. Subtle variation in the texture and color of fabrics creates a quiet and nuanced look.

If you love something that goes against conventional wisdom, don't be afraid to try it. Maybe you believe that you can never mix too many florals or that there's no such thing as overkill with plaid, and that's okay. Do what makes you smile when you come home; just know why you're doing it. The very best homes are those that are extremely personal and surprising, which always requires a little rule-breaking (see Chapter 19, on Risk and Confidence).

FABRIC GUIDE

FABRIC	DESCRIPTION	USES
LINEN	Made from flax, linen has a natural wrinkle to it that gives a room a relaxed, natural, lived-in feel. It can be heavy or lightweight, and it gets softer and better with age.	Upholstery, slipcovers, curtains (lined or unlined), pillows, bedding. **CHAIR, PAGE 90**
CHINTZ	Chintz is, to quote my husband's fraternity motto, "loved or hated but never ignored." Though it is often a controversial fabric, I can't help loving a good chintz. People received an overdose of chintz from heavily "chintzed" rooms of the 1980s; a little bit of chintz goes a long way. Chintz doesn't need to be taken seriously. I prefer it in small doses, such as on a single piece of upholstery or a pillow, but at times it makes sense to apply it to multiple pieces of furniture.	Upholstery, slipcovers, curtains (lined), pillows, walls. **FLORAL CHAIRS, PAGE 112**
HEMP	Hemp is similar to linen, though typically slightly rougher in feel. I adore hemp.	Upholstery, slipcovers, curtains (lined or unlined), pillows. **DINING CHAIRS, PAGE 21**
INDOOR-OUTDOOR FABRICS	There are many different brands to consider when looking at indoor-outdoor fabrics, and they work just as well inside as they do outside. They're great for banquettes and high-use pieces with families with kids and pets. My living room sofa, which takes a serious beating from our four children, is a white indoor-outdoor linen blend. Not all indoor-outdoor fabrics are created equal, however, so it's best to take a swatch of the fabric home, do your worst to it, and see what happens. I rubbed oily tomato sauce all over my white fabric swatch and made sure it washed out before I decided to go ahead with it.	Upholstery, slipcovers. **WHITE SOFA, PAGE 23**
SILK	Spun by silkworms, silk is one of the most beautiful and delicate of fabrics. When you're looking to add deep and vibrant color to a space, silk is one of the best fabrics to choose, because it's available in such highly saturated colors. It lasts best on pieces that will not be heavily used.	Curtains (with blackout lining, so the sun doesn't fade it), pillows. **CURTAINS, PAGE 124**
VELVET	Luxurious and cozy, velvet is also available in extremely saturated colors with a stunning luminosity, so it's often used to bring depth and richness to a room. I love taking naps on my velvet sofa. On non-velvet sofas, I often add a soft velvet throw pillow for naps.	Upholstery, curtains (blackout lined to prevent fading), pillows. **SOFAS, PAGE 116**
VINYL	Faux leathers have come a long way—some are difficult to distinguish from leather. They are available in a variety of shiny to matte finishes. Since vinyl is practical and cleanable, harsher chemicals can often be used on it, so there is less to worry about.	Heavy-use upholstery, dining banquettes. **DINING CHAIRS, PAGES 56–57**
WOOL	Wool is soft and quiet and has a masculine feel. Typical patterns for wool are plaids, herringbones, and stripes. Solid felted wool is one of my favorite upholstery materials.	Upholstery, curtains, pillows, bedding, and walls. **BED, PAGE 162**
LEATHER	Obviously, leather isn't a "fabric" but is often used in the same ways we use fabric. Durable and practical, it becomes "broken in" over time and gets better with age. Take care to moisturize leather every year or so with a leather conditioner so that it doesn't dry out and crack.	Heavy-use upholstery. **OTTOMAN, PAGE 171**
TWILL/DENIM	Twill and denim are washable and stain-resistant, so I use them on kid-friendly upholstery and pieces that will see a lot of wear, such as window seats. They wash well and make hardy slipcovers. When considering going very light or white on upholstery, either twill or denim is a great choice.	Upholstery, pillows. **WINDOW SEAT CUSHION, PAGE 141**

CHAPTER 8

LIGHTING

$$\left\{ \begin{array}{c} \text{light·ing / līt'-iŋ – n.} \\ \text{a giving of light or of being lighted; illumination; ignition} \end{array} \right\}$$

Opposite: In this grand traditional foyer, my client was looking for a bit of the unexpected, and to be reminded of the light-filled homes of Hawaii, where she grew up. Inspired by Japanese fishing floats, we selected a pair of oversize blown-glass orb bunches for the ceiling.

I'M A NATURAL-LIGHT FIEND, so during the day, I rely on sunlight, and we don't turn on the lights in our house until it's dark. We use candles at dinner in the cool months as much as possible, because every occasion feels more special with them. We have lights for functional needs and lights that make our home cozy. My living room isn't properly lit right now, because my young boys have broken a few table lamps, and I'm waiting a little bit before subjecting more lamps to them. Even though we have overhead lighting, task lighting, and lots of nearby ambient lighting, I miss those broken lamps. The room has dark spots at night where they belong.

Three general types of lighting are needed in each space: ambient, task, and accent lighting. Chandeliers, ceiling fixtures, lamps, and wall lighting produce good general lighting, or ambient lighting, that's necessary in any given space. Directional lamps provide task light for activities such as reading or writing, and pendants provide task lighting for countertops or tables. Art lights, bookshelf lights, under-cabinet lighting, and directional spotlights are used to accentuate interesting features in a room and to create atmosphere. Be sure to place all lighting on dimmers so that you can control the brightness and, ultimately, the mood in every room of the house. A surprisingly large amount of lighting is required for a properly lit room. It's not uncommon to have six to fifteen different sources of light in a single room.

I generally avoid recessed lighting in rooms made for relaxing, because it simply isn't flattering to people. Never place it directly above where people's heads will be, such as over a seating area, because it can look and feel like an interrogation lamp. The best use of recessed lighting is over the walkways in a kitchen, but even this can be avoided with small flush-mount fixtures that can also do the job. Especially avoid recessed lighting in the bedroom and living room, where lamplight is the most comfortable and flattering illumination. Also be careful of directional lighting from above, as it can have the same effect.

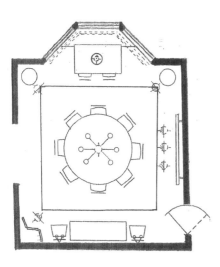

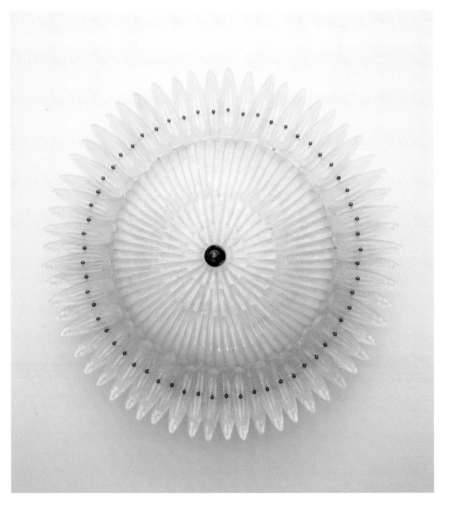

Above, left: A lighting plan.

Above, right: One of a pair of massive statement-making vintage murano glass chandeliers in our clients' foyer.

Opposite: Sculptural brass art lights over built-in shelving add interest during the day and illuminate the shelves and objects with a soft glow at night.

The key to properly lighting a room is thinking through every possible scenario and envisioning what type of light will be needed. Imagine yourself in each situation, and think about where the light should come from. Will it be too bright? Too direct? Too dim? For example, in a kitchen, think of each task you'll need to perform: cooking at the range, chopping food on the island and countertops, doing dishes at the sink, seeing the floor when you sweep, emptying the dishwasher, eating at the table, and so on. Each of these tasks requires specific types of lighting. Your selection process becomes simple when you take the time to think it through, and it will have a huge effect on the overall space. I know that whenever a lightbulb goes out in my kitchen, I miss it dearly in the few days it takes us to replace it.

Once you've done a mental or physical walk-through of your entire home and have figured out exactly what types of lighting you will need, you can go about shopping for the lights—the fun part! And, if your house is anything like mine, and you've got some dark spots at night that keep it from feeling just right, think about how you can fix them. I'm hoping to address my lamp-less living room any day now!

GENERAL LIGHTING GUIDELINES

FOYERS: A central fixture overhead in the foyer helps set the tone for the rest of the home. Depending upon space, it can be a large or small hanging fixture or a flush-mount. If the foyer is large enough, a table lamp or sconces (or both!) add a welcoming glow.

DINING ROOMS: Dining rooms need a central chandelier (or two if it's an extremely long table) hung 29–33 inches above the table, a lamp or two (or a pair of sconces) on a sideboard, along with candlelight on the table at night. Artwork and/or hutches may need additional accent lighting, which can add a charming glow to the room.

LIVING ROOMS & FAMILY ROOMS: Light all four corners of the room; use accent lighting where possible, a central fixture if applicable, and task lighting wherever needed. Larger rooms will need additional lighting in the center so they don't feel dark. If lighting is needed on a floating piece of furniture, such as a console in the center of the room, getting the plug to an electrical outlet can be tricky. We typically install an outlet in the floor under the piece of furniture and cut a hole through the rug to the outlet. We prefer not to cut through antique or vintage rugs, though, so in this case use a natural-fiber rug.

KITCHENS: Place pendants over an island (approximately 33–34 inches above the countertop) and a ceiling fixture over the table in the eating area. Add accent lighting under the range hood and cabinets if applicable. Steer clear of bluish-looking lights; aim for warm light. I like lighting over a sink and prefer wall-washers of some sort in the kitchen to highlight cabinetry or shelving at night. I often resort to recessed lighting over the walkways of kitchens. A beautiful alternative is surface-mounted fixtures that give overall light.

BEDROOMS: Place lamps on the nightstands, a lamp or two on a dresser, and a central ceiling fixture if applicable, though I often prefer a ceiling fan (with no light) for nighttime breezes.

BATHROOMS: Start with a central ceiling fixture for overall lighting, add task lighting beside (not above) the mirror if possible, and recessed lighting in the shower if needed. If you need to install your vanity lighting above the mirror, make sure that the overall lighting in the room is bright enough so the vanity lights don't cast unflattering shadows on the face.

SHADE OPTIONS

The material of a shade strongly affects how its light is cast.

FABRIC: Pleasing to look at. Available in multiple colors. Wonderful for table and floor lamps and hanging fixtures.

CLEAR GLASS: Attractive. Can be difficult to look at directly. Best for above eye level.

METAL: Use for directional lighting. Good-looking but can cast sharp light that feels a bit like "interrogation room" lighting. Can become hot to the touch. Best for task lighting, reading lamps, art lamps, island pendants.

PAPER: Pleasing to the eye. Casual, relaxed. Wonderful for table and floor lamps and hanging fixtures.

WHITE GLASS: Nice overall lighting that can be looked at directly. Works well in bathrooms and kitchens.

PORCELAIN: Use for directional lighting. Can cast sharp "interrogation room" beam of light. Best for task lighting.

Left: A brass sconce with paper shades illuminates a pair of miniature paintings in a hallway. I typically have the center of the sconce hung approximately five feet high, except in narrow hallways or stairways, where I'll often raise them to around six feet.

CHAPTER 9

WINDOW TREATMENTS

{
win·dow / win'-dō – n.
an opening in a building, vehicle, or container, for letting
in light or air or for looking through
}

Opposite: Silk shades and linen curtains add layers and softness to the sitting area of a master bedroom.

I BELIEVE THE INDOOR-OUTDOOR CONNECTION in a home is vital, and because windows and doors are that gateway, the type of window treatment, if any, to be used in a room is an important consideration. If a view is stunning, the window itself is beautiful, there is no need for privacy, and the room itself feels warm enough and isn't lacking in fabrics, I will forgo window treatments. It's not often, however, that all these stars align, so I'm also a fan of classic, simple window treatments: curtain panels with rods and rings, Roman shades, roller shades, and shutters.

I use floor-to-ceiling curtain panels in most cases because they make the room feel taller and airier, they add a beautiful layer of fabric in a room, and they can also make up for lackluster architecture. The curtain fabrics and the style of curtain panel, the pleating, trim, and hardware all affect the level of formality in a room. Pleated curtains are more formal, whereas straight panels are more casual. Likewise, lined silk and velvet curtains feel the most formal, whereas unlined linens and cottons are casual.

GUIDELINES FOR NON-PLEATED/ FLAT-PANEL WIDTH

20"–30" WINDOWS: a pair of single panels, 50 inches each

30"–48" WINDOWS: a pair of 1.5' or double panels, 75 to 100 inches each

48"–84" WINDOWS: a pair of double panels, 100 inches each

84"–144" WINDOWS: a pair of triple panels, 150 inches with possible quadruple panels (200 inches) if a fuller look is desired

CALCULATING PANEL WIDTHS

One of the trickiest things to calculate is the proper number of panel widths for a window. Standard single-curtain panel widths are approximately fifty inches, because most fabric comes fifty-four inches wide, which allows for seaming. You should be able to pull two curtain panels easily shut without their going taut. On a typical thirty-three-inch-wide window, use a pair of double-width (one hundred inches of fabric) pleated panels or two single-and-a-half-width (seventy-five inches of fabric) non-pleated panels for a full look. The guidelines to the left will help you calculate required panel widths, and are based on non-pleated panels. For pleated panels, add an extra half panel (twenty-five inches) to full panel (fifty inches) for every single panel of width.

CURTAIN LENGTH

A tailored curtain should just touch, or "kiss," the floor but never hover above it. For a slightly less tailored look, allow a two- to four-inch break of curtain fabric on the floor. For a romantic look, allow the panels to go even longer so that they puddle on the floor.

TO LINE OR NOT TO LINE?

For lighter-colored fabrics that aren't at risk of fading, I often specify unlined curtains, which have a casual, relaxed, airy feel. For bright or saturated colors, and especially silks or velvets, to protect against fading from the sun, it's safest to use blackout lining behind the fabrics. Be sure to keep curtains clear of dust, with regular shaking out and/or vacuuming, because the sun on the dust particles can make the fabric brittle very quickly. A lined curtain feels more formal, whereas an unlined curtain is casual.

CURTAIN HARDWARE

For curtain hardware, I typically like the emphasis to be on the fabric rather than the hardware, so I use simple, thin rods and rings in both formal and casual homes. On flat, non-pleated panels, I like ten rings per panel, and on pleated panels, I prefer seven rings per single panel.

ROMAN SHADES

Roman shades, which fold into themselves, can be made from fabric or natural woven materials. Roman shades work beautifully on their own—in kitchens, bathrooms, and children's rooms—as well as in conjunction with curtains for a pretty, layered look. When ordering, specify "inside mount" for shades that will mount inside the window frame, and "outside mount" for those that will mount on or outside the window frame. When the woodwork on a window frame is particularly interesting or beautiful, I opt for inside mount shades. If the woodwork is nothing to speak of or I'm worried about blocking light, I specify outside mount shades, because they can be affixed to the trim or even higher to reduce the amount of shade that blocks the window when the shade is up. I frequently use natural woven shades or matchstick shades to bring an additional natural element to a room. Unlined matchstick shades filter light nicely but are see-through at night, so if privacy is needed, line them.

ROLLER SHADES

Roller shades are ideal for a simple, no-fuss look. (See page 151.) They work well alone or paired with curtains. These use inside mounts.

SHUTTERS

Shutters can offer a fresh, clean look. They're also ideal in spaces where moisture might become an issue for fabrics, such as bathrooms. Indoor shutters have louvers that can open and close; though, even when the louvers are open, your view to the outdoors is generally inhibited.

WOODEN BLINDS

Wooden blinds are ideal for areas in which little ornamentation is needed and they should be inset into the window. They can be pulled up so that the view out the window is completely unhindered and pulled down for complete privacy.

RECIPE FOR THE PERFECT WINDOW

My go-to window treatment entails mounting curtain hardware at the ceiling or just under the crown molding. Roman shades should hang just below that hardware, mounted above the window and outside the trim; outside mount to allow as much of the window as possible to show and to give the illusion that the window continues higher, which visually heightens the entire room. This treatment is both functional and beautiful, because the curtain panels remain stationary, while the Roman shades go up and down for privacy, and you now have two opportunities to add texture and pattern to a room instead of just one. I'm especially partial to unlined linen curtains; I love how the light shines through them and how relaxed and natural they look.

CHAPTER 10

ART & ACCESSORIES

{
art / ärt – n.

products of creative work; paintings, statues, etc.

ac·ces·so·ry / ək'-ses-ər-ē – n.

something extra; thing added to help in a secondary way
}

Opposite: A sculptor's stand with a bust that was actually sculpted on it sits at the end of a mezzanine overlooking a living room.

EACH AND EVERY ITEM THAT GOES INTO A HOUSE is an intricate part of a fully finished home, but the art and accessories, the final layer of living, offer perhaps the greatest opportunity to inject personality and meaning into a home. When we decorate a home, we select artwork and accessories that will remain fairly constant throughout the seasons, make us happy, and mean something to us. We incorporate our passions and interests into our home through the objects and collections we display.

However, the way a room is "styled"—the manner in which art, accessories, tabletops, bookshelves, flowers, and food are arranged—can completely change its mood. When we decorate for a holiday, for example, we could be said to be "styling" for Thanksgiving or Christmas. The general decorating with the furniture, rugs, or window treatments may remain the same, but the accents can change. We may swap a painting over the mantel for a wreath, use special china on the dining table, and do seasonal arrangements around the house.

Each shelter magazine styles the homes it shoots and has its own aesthetic, which readers have come to expect. Magazines will rearrange furniture and bring in flower arrangements and a variety of accessories, including pillows, bedding, and tabletop items. Just as the magazines use this ever-important layer to create a mood and a vibe, so should we in our own homes. When we reach the accessorizing stage, it's truly time to get personal. Our accessories should reflect our personal tastes. A sophisticated home can still be playful, fun, and quirky; it doesn't need to take itself too seriously. While we may not have a "fun" sofa or a "happy" coffee table, incorporating a collection of photography on a lighthearted topic can add cheerfulness and communicate your personality.

Above, left: The painting by mid-century artist Ernest Springer in our dining room is a conversation starter. The old printers' trays on the wall to the right are full of nature finds we've collected on walks in the woods. Above the printers' trays I nailed sheets of beautiful bark we found in our wanderings.

Above, right: A client's striking collection of Buddhas.

Personally, I have a thing for portraits of men, mostly old men. I cannot pass up an affordable, well-done painting of a timeworn face with an interesting expression. I didn't realize that I was "collecting" these paintings until I looked around a few years ago and saw just how many we had. Now, whenever we're out antiquing and David sees one, he calls out, "I found another old man!" We continue to collect these anonymous portraits because they're intriguing to us and they make us smile. Friends often ask us about them—especially about the one in our dining room of a younger man with pigeons—and we have fun making up stories. We're not serious art aficionados, but we buy what we love and what makes us happy, which is the best advice I can offer to anyone uncertain about buying art. Our portrait collection is odd and a definite quirk in our house, but it's also part of what makes it unique and makes it "us."

THE ARRANGEMENT OF THINGS

Above: Our clients' tiered glass coffee table showcases books, accessories, and natural objects.

The actual arrangement of our possessions and how many of them we use determines whether or not our home feels cluttered, sterile, showroom-y, hodgepodged, or perfectly lived-in. My goal when arranging accessories is to create a space that doesn't feel overstyled or overedited or cluttered. This goes back to the "pace" of a room and how "busy" you want it to be. I like just enough stuff to keep a room interesting, but not so much that I can't think in the place, which is entirely subjective, I realize. The only places I make an exception for are bookshelves, because I love a cluttered bookshelf jammed with both books and objects.

COLLECT OVER TIME

My family likes to collect natural objects during walks. If we go to the beach, we hunt for shells, fossils, coral, and driftwood, and if it's a walk around our neighborhood, we pick up whatever's in season, whether it's flowers, plants, acorns, or seed pods, and sometimes even pretty pebbles or butterfly wings. The kids love coming home and loading up the nature boxes, and when I look at the boxes, I'm reminded of good times. Accessories should be things that interest us, or things that we find beautiful, meaningful, or funny. Never buy "stuff" just to fill up space, which makes for a boring, uninspired look.

It can be challenging to accessorize a home when starting from scratch. Some of us may be just beginning our decorating journey and have only a few special, loved possessions, and some of us may even have nothing at all. How do we develop a meaningful collection of things rather than instantaneously filling our home with trendy impulse purchases from big-box stores?

In my own home, I like to mix newer pieces with older ones. For example, in the kitchen, I use vintage tableware and antique ironstone and sturdy, hand-blown drinking glasses, along with basic and practical pieces from chain retail stores such as Pottery Barn or Target, and, overall, it looks as if it's been collected over time, even though I have new pieces mixed in.

When accessorizing a home, I take my time looking for the right unique, vintage, antique, or handmade pieces with patina and character as opposed to new items sold by national retailers. The best places to search for interesting finds are vintage and antiques shops, flea markets, thrift stores, interior design boutiques, and online marketplaces such as eBay, Etsy, 1stdibs, and One Kings Lane. Whenever I'm shopping either in a store or online and find something unique that I love on first sight, that I can afford, or that will fit in my car, I buy it. I'm not always exactly sure where it will go, but I know I'll find a home for it if I love it. I encourage you to do the same thing. If you come across something you love and don't have a specific place in mind for it, go for it anyway—as long as your home isn't already filled with stuff—because you will figure out the right spot for it. Over time, this is how a home begins to feel "collected." To the left is a list of the things I typically buy new versus old (though some might overlap). Whenever possible, for the sake of the environment, it's best to buy old or used over new.

THE LIVE ELEMENT

When I'm working on a room design in my head, I often envision the room complete with potted plants or certain types of flowers in vases, because to me, that "live," organic element is an essential part of most spaces. A room doesn't feel quite right to me without a little bit of life in it. Also, I find I can never have enough vases. I like to have a wide variety of interesting ones around for casual

GOOD THINGS TO BUY NEW
Bed pillows, bedding, throw blankets, soft goods, rugs, trays, artisan-made goods and handmade items, baskets and organizational items, lamp shades, everyday dishes and glasses, art, sculpture, photography, books, upholstery, window treatments.

GOOD THINGS TO BUY OLD
Decorative objects, vases, antique or vintage fabrics to be made into throw pillows or curtains, table linens, rugs, trays, baskets, silver, tableware, serving ware, unique glasses, candlesticks, art, sculpture, mirrors, photographs, casegoods, odd chairs, books, lighting, hardware.

Above: Antique Belgian bowls in the kitchen are simple and practical yet beautiful even when not in use.

greenery and flower arrangements. Never pass up an affordable vase you love. They also make wonderful gifts, because, although many homes are stocked with clear and crystal vases, the typical household can always use another interesting or beautiful "statement" vase.

BEAUTY IN THE EVERYDAY

You should have a preference for or a connection with almost everything you bring into your home. We need many things for practical purposes—dishes, glasses, napkins, soap, laundry baskets—but these things should also be aesthetically pleasing to us. If you have to buy something, make sure it's your favorite of its kind. The more attractive items sometimes cost a bit more, but it's always worth it in the long run if you only have to buy something once and you keep it forever because you love it. Beautiful everyday items are some of the most interesting, especially when arranged creatively. Cutting boards can become works of art when proudly displayed in a kitchen, and simple pitchers and glasses make a statement when stored or put to use out in the open.

MEANINGFUL WALLS

Fill your walls with meaningful pieces rather than "filler." Don't buy just to fill space. Good art doesn't have to be expensive. There are many artists doing shows and selling their work online at very good prices. Etsy is one of my favorite sources for original art and photography. You can also buy illustrated books, tear out your favorite images, frame them, and hang them like artwork.

Look at your available wall space so that you know approximately how much you need to fill it. Remember, you don't need to fill all empty space. This is where your elevations (page 43) will come in handy. It helps to have your sketches with dimensions when you're shopping so you know your size parameters. You can sketch various different-size frames on the elevation to determine what will work best. What is placed on a wall should generally be of a similar scale to the empty wall itself so that it fits well in the space.

Above, left: Fresh chard and herbs from the garden are elevated into beautiful arrangements when stored in a collection of glass pitchers on the kitchen counter. The herbs stay fresh and add bright green beauty to the kitchen while they're waiting to be used. No need to hide them away in the refrigerator!

Above, right: Everyday wineglasses look artful when arranged in a wall niche.

Above: A sideboard displays old, collected objects to create a monochromatic vignette in a family room.

With art and accessories, the bottom line is, if something holds meaning for you and you love it, then you can find a way to make it work. Never buy something just because it's a good deal. When buying, ask yourself if you'll still like it in five years or twenty. If the answer isn't yes and you don't need it, then reconsider. (The exception to this is a variety of soft goods like pillows, curtains, and bedding, which won't always last ten or twenty years.) When you're buying a lot all at once, the temptation to cut corners will be strong, but when all the dust settles and things slow down, you'll most likely come to regret those cut corners. Be patient and take it slow. You don't need to buy everything at once. You can fill your new spaces slowly over time. Buy only what you love and what works toward the ultimate vision you've devised for your home. When I look back at the purchases I regret, most of them were impulse buys. It's the things I've methodically and patiently collected over time that I plan on keeping, like my old men—I'll keep them until their faces don't feel so old to me anymore.

HANGING ART

Art should be hung or displayed at an average person's eye level for optimal viewing. When hanging art above a sofa, allow approximately six to twelve inches between the back of the sofa and the bottom of the artwork so that there is space for people's heads. When hanging pieces on the wall, whether it's a single item or a grouping, look to place items of a similar shape and

THE SIMPLE STATEMENT

Sometimes all that's needed is a single piece of art over a mantel, a sofa, a dresser, or a bed.

THE BIG STATEMENT

Use large-scale pieces to make a statement. This photograph of a horse is of a very similar proportion to the wall and it fits perfectly.

THE GRID

An art collection displayed in the form of a grid creates a beautiful focal point. The framed photographs above these chairs are pages torn from the vintage German magazine *The Manipulator*. I had them hung so that they dipped slightly below the tops of the wing chairs to create a cozier, layered look in an otherwise very airy and modern space. This technique brings the eye downward and grounds it. I have done this with a single piece of art as well.

scale together. For example, if an open wall area is taller than it is wide, hang something of a similar proportion to fill in the vertical space. Likewise, go with linear arrangements when the wall space is linear. When art doesn't fit the space, it can look awkward or feel unfinished. When a space is filled in properly, a room feels more permanent, balanced, and purposeful.

SALON-STYLE GALLERY WALLS

Salon-style gallery walls feel collected and lend energy to a space. They can be added to and tweaked over time, so they're a wonderful choice for those who are continually adding to their collections. When I do gallery walls like the one above, I don't plan them out perfectly until I'm actually hanging the art in the room. I may do a sketch of the general idea, but nothing is ever exactly as planned. I arrange it all generally on the floor and then start nailing it into the walls. You can look online for some techniques for the perfect gallery wall—using templates, brown paper bags, etc.—but I prefer to wing it and go with what feels and looks best to me. I typically do pieces one and a half to two and a half inches apart from one another on a gallery wall. Clients are often shocked by the number of pieces needed to fill an entire wall. It can be an expensive proposition. The gallery wall in my bedroom (above) took more than thirty pieces of art and we still have more room to grow.

FILLING IN THE BLANKS

There are instances when it's best to simply fill in the blanks with art or accessories. Artwork or sconces work well above chairs.

DECORATE WITH OBJECTS

Not everything that goes onto a wall has to be a piece of art or mirrors. Certain objects make interesting and dramatic statements. My dad found this old cypress tree root thirty years ago while fishing, and I love it for its natural, sculptural appeal, and also because it reminds me of my dad.

PART 2

THE INTANGIBLE ELEMENTS OF DESIGN, OR *JE NE SAIS QUOI*

{ **je ne sais quoi (uncountable)**
an intangible quality that makes something distinctive or attractive }

Much good design comes from logic, careful planning, and attention to color, scale, and harmony. But another part relies on intuition and an intimate understanding of elements that are rather intangible. A home's ultimate success relies upon being able to create an atmosphere that brings about a desired emotional response. This section is about using those intangible elements to elicit certain emotions and moods.

Opposite: Lively pattern and bold color mix in this formal living room. Architecture by Franck & Lohsen.

CHAPTER 11

AESTHETIC

{ **aes·thet·ic** / es·thet′·ik – n.
a set of principles underlying and guiding the work
of a particular artist or artistic movement }

AN AESTHETIC IS THE SET OF UNDERLYING PRINCIPLES that guides the work of an artist. In other words, it is what the artist thinks of as "good." When we undertake any sort of creative endeavor, *we* become the artist, and each decision we make is ultimately based upon *our* aesthetic, our principles, or what we consider "good." Getting to know one's aesthetic is the keystone to making any sort of design decision.

We are each inherently and uniquely drawn to what we find beautiful or interesting, which then forms our personal aesthetic. Learning what embodies beauty can be a lifelong process, and our tastes evolve as we are exposed to new things and experiences. The more we're able to understand our own personal aesthetic, the easier it is to express in the design of a home.

Opposite: A spare, serene bedroom in the mountains.

Imagine the same field of wildflowers painted by three different artists: da Vinci, Monet, and Picasso. The three paintings would look vastly different from one another, because each artist had a unique aesthetic.

The same thing is true in home decor. Three decorators, each with a strong aesthetic, will appeal to very different people. Even if they're each designing a formal living room in similar shades of blue, each room will be distinct.

Think about people you are familiar with who have very recognizable aesthetics: designers such as Kelly Wearstler, Ralph Lauren, or Thomas O'Brien; fashion icons and brands such as Chanel or Anthropologie; or maybe even your stylish best friend. These are people and companies who understand what they like and what they value, and they have the confidence to convey it—whether through their dress, their homes, their art, their work, their products, or their marketing materials. They have a unique look or brand, and everything they do underscores their aesthetic.

Each and every one of us can develop an aesthetic strong enough to shine through in a variety of settings, styles, and media if we concentrate on what we value and then make creative choices to convey it.

The living rooms on the previous pages are incredibly different in style, yet if you look closely, they share a similar aesthetic.

Somehow, there is a connection between the rooms: The hand is very similar; there's a similar pace; the balance of the furnishings and the pattern-to-solid ratio is similar, resulting in an overall impression of breathing room. Natural elements are woven throughout (the sisal and jute rugs, the massive sea sponge, the marble grapes, the fiddle-leaf fig, the rustic wood pieces, the ferns from the mountain, and a substantial amount of linen). Both spaces blend periods and styles, which makes the rooms feel timeless and collected. And though their styles are very different—Louis XVI elegance, polished and formal versus rustic, casual, and a bit vintage—the key underlying aesthetic is the same.

Think about what is essentially "you" in every situation, and let the rest of the superficial things go, including style factors (for example, "Mid-Century" or "Hollywood Glam"). What's left is your aesthetic.

Our aesthetics are ever-evolving and often elusive; however, the more we verbalize or express them, the stronger they become (and we become more confident in creative decision-making, too).

So, how do you discover your aesthetic? You can find inspiration all around you—in fashion, art, music, nature, the food you enjoy, movies and books you love, and, of course, homes you admire. Collect your ideas in one place (a folder with photos from magazines or an online pinboard), and take note of what attracts you. Look for themes, similarities, or patterns that run through the things you've collected. Eventually, you'll have little aesthetic epiphanies, helping you realize the key principles that are fundamental to your aesthetic.

Write down a list of these principles that you value, a list of what is "good" to you. If that seems too daunting, start with simple words you would use to describe styles you like: *simple, complex, colorful, muted, monochromatic, natural, formal, relaxed, realistic, emotional, eclectic, minimal, classic, modern, traditional, cute, sophisticated, feminine, masculine, crisp, erudite, old-fashioned, quirky, unique, edgy, soft, harsh, strong, romantic, fun, timeless.* For example, Ralph Lauren's style is classic, strong, timeless, American, and is known for its quality. Ralph Lauren's aesthetic is the set of principles that guide his style. It could be described as:

Classic and timelessness are paramount.
Quality is key.
A pride in American style is evident.

Now, using the list of words, make statements that describe your aesthetic.

Above: In a lake house bedroom, a low, modern bed upholstered in charcoal linen mixes with vintage blue batik textiles and natural materials that evoke the water just outside the door.

Opposite: In our dining room, an inset vintage wine rack with minimal trim, rustic bench below it, linen chair, metal table, and basket of wildflowers combine to express our aesthetic.

For help in figuring out your own aesthetic, refer to the Filters Work Sheet on page 270.

As you begin to make decisions and selections in designing your home, use these statements to make sure you're being true to your aesthetic. Defining our own aesthetics is the key to choosing between what we truly like and what we think we should bring into our homes. There's so much "good" out there, but your aesthetic determines what is, ultimately, "you."

CHAPTER 12

STYLE

style / stīl – n.
a specific or characteristic manner of expression, execution, construction, or design,
in any art, period, work, employment, physical appearance, etc.
a distinctive appearance, typically determined by the principles (aesthetic)
according to which something is designed

THE MOST SUCCESSFUL HOMES reflect the people who live there, revealing their passions and points of view, and these homes are much more inspiring than those that are simply stylish or pretty. Style is a direct manifestation of aesthetic: It's the result of applied aesthetic principles. It is the appearance or output, in a particular context, of an aesthetic.

Opposite: A corner of our master bedroom with a natural, textural, 1970s vibe.

There are the many familiar styles—traditional, mid-century modern, Louis XVI, preppy, boho, classic, Colonial, rustic, glamorous, and thousands of others—and then there is personal style, which may combine broader styles or exist on its own. A building itself might have a certain architectural style, and the occupant has a personal style and aesthetic, and these are both essential considerations in designing a home.

My own aesthetic blends natural elements with styles both old and new, plus an ample amount of breathing room. At times this manifests as a style with a rustic, 1970s edge, as in my own home, and at other times it appears to be a more formal, classic, and refined style, as in the home on the following pages.

Style isn't one-size-fits-all. If you take an authentic approach to decorating, your style will vary slightly in each home you design, because the architecture, landscape, and neighborhood setting all have an influence. (Whereas your aesthetic, though possibly evolving, remains more of a constant.) If you put your personal style into words and then put your home's style into words, the resulting list can help determine a "vocabulary" for the project.

Here is an example from the home on the following pages. When I begin with a client, I put his or her style into words: *glamorous, sophisticated, fun, colorful, bold, artsy, sparkly, luxurious, modern.*

And then I write down the house's style: *classic, traditional, formal, refined, graceful, historic.*

Above: An oversize modern settee upholstered in a traditional China blue chintz by Schumacker sits at one end of my clients' formal living room. Glowy green silk curtains and velvet slipper chairs contrast with pale blue walls and cobalt sofas. Architecture by Franck & Lohsen.

What results is a language for the project and possibly for a marriage of styles; it's also the "filter" (see Filters Work Sheet on page 270) through which all things that come into the home must pass:

> *classic yet fun, historic and traditional bones with modern touches, graceful and glamorous, sparkly and luxurious, sophisticated and refined, bold, colorful, and artsy.*

As I search for the pieces of the puzzle—the fabrics, the furnishings, the paint colors, the accessories—making decisions becomes simple and logical. Only items that meet the list's (or "filter's") requirements (along with my own established aesthetic principles, to make sure that every item is in keeping with the full vision) will make it into the final design.

Above: The newly renovated foyer in the same home offers a first glimpse at the chic, vibrant colors and glamour of the rest of the house.

Like discoveries in a treasure hunt, everything for the project on these pages fell into place at just the right time, resulting in a fresh mix of eras and provenances that completely expresses my clients' style. On a trip to a New Orleans antiques store, I came across a set of four antique blue grisailles (near-monochromatic paintings used in imitation of sculpture) that were rescued from the walls of a French Provincial manor house just before the French Revolution. I loved their color, depth, and patina, and I thought the set might be just the thing for my clients' foyer walls. The lot of antique marble tiles tracked down by one of our tile reps also happened to fit perfectly with the floor pattern we had designed. The pair of Murano-glass chandeliers is mid-century, and the foyer table is an English antique, both of which were just the right dimensions and style for the space.

Right: In the same home, a pair of back-to-back cobalt blue velvet chesterfield sofas separates the expansive living room into two comfortable conversation groupings.

CHAPTER 13

MOOD

mood / müd – n
1. a particular state of mind or feeling
2. a predominant or pervading feeling, spirit, or tone }

ONCE A HOME HAS MET ALL OF OUR PHYSICAL NEEDS, we look to it to make us feel good and to bring us comfort and a sense of security. We ask more from a house than simply shelter. We want our homes to make us feel a certain way, and to do this, our house needs to have a "mood."

Opposite: Vintage bottles sit atop the deep window ledge in a farmhouse.

Your home's atmosphere should represent a conscious choice. Think about how you want to feel when you're in it, how you want others to feel, and how the house itself needs to "feel" so that people in it will respond accordingly. We bring to the "decorating table," so to speak, our own aesthetic and personal style. A sports lover might choose to have athletic equipment, photos, and trophies visible in the living room; a romantic-art lover would have a different idea. In all of us, different things stimulate different emotions.

When I'm at home, I like to feel relaxed, happy, creative, and free. I'm almost always barefoot. I want my house to make me feel a certain way, to put me in a certain mood. For each emotion, certain physical and aesthetic requirements must be met. What I need to feel creative is lots of white, open space. I feel freer to think and dream when I'm not encountering a lot of visual stimulation, clutter, and color. Because of this, my house needs to be open and airy and fairly neutral-colored and clutter-free to make room for all the activity and mess of daily life. I love "cozy" as much as anybody else, but I need open space to really feel good at home.

Everything, though rarely where it should be, has its place, which makes living easy and organized. We play music all the time, try to stay stocked with good food and drinks, have lots of comfy places to flop, and like to light candles or the fire whenever we can. All of this makes me happy, and I feel free to be completely me.

Keep in mind that different rooms of a house often call for slightly different moods. I mentioned that I like my home to feel light, airy, and open, yet in my dining room, which is small and dark, I embraced a sort of intimate, cozy atmosphere, which is conducive to long dinners and conversations and very different from the rest of the house. I love a small, cozy space to dine in, but I need something totally different in general living areas.

}128 HABITAT

Above: In this formal living room, our goal was to create a thoughtful, somewhat moody space for our clients, where they could sit by the fire and talk or play the piano, which is just outside this shot in the right-hand corner.

Once you've established the desired mood for a home and all the rooms in it, evaluate each choice in terms of that mood. Every item you put into a home will affect its mood—fabrics, lighting, furniture, art, and accessories—so always ask yourself if the item you're considering is in keeping with the desired mood. Will this coffee table make the room feel fresh and fun or formal and romantic? Is the lighting too serious or formal?

Color is one of the most significant factors affecting mood. Because color causes immediate subconscious emotional responses in most people, I often begin with a color palette. I'll select key fabrics, rugs, or art first and consider wall color before shopping for specific pieces of furniture. For example, I'll pick a sofa fabric before I decide upon the actual sofa frame.

It's important to figure out exactly what mood you want your home to have. A mood could be any one of the following: happy, cheerful, fresh, formal, casual, romantic, cozy, airy, warm, thoughtful, moody, vibrant, relaxed, exciting, stimulating, fun, low-key, calm, light, or dark.

Above: Having lived on a boat for a time when they were younger and spending their travels visiting coastal areas, my clients absolutely love the water and wanted to be reminded of it in their home. Materials such as seagrass, rope, and driftwood, as well as a palette of sandy tones and soft blues and greens, allude to the coast, put them at ease, and make them happy.

Once again, I find that writing things down is incredibly helpful in ultimately achieving real, tangible goals. Figuring out the "language" of a project is key. You can use your project language to aid in decision-making, answering questions, and to communicate with others involved in the project, such as architects, designers, contractors, salespeople, or artisans. For each new project, I put on the proverbial "project glasses," and I make all decisions through that perspective, or with those glasses on, so to speak. So put on your own "colored" glasses whenever you begin to decorate your home.

I've created a Filters Work Sheet (see page 270) that will help you define your overall vision, which will aid you throughout the process of designing your home. This may seem daunting at first, but it can be broken down into a series of logical steps: searching for inspiration, asking yourself key questions, and doing a little bit of design soul-searching. Once you've articulated who you are (your aesthetic and style), the style of home you want, and its mood, you'll have everything you need to decorate deeply and authentically.

Right: My dad wanted his lake house to be a place where we could all gather as a family to relax and enjoy being together. I wanted the house to have a strong sense of place: The mood in the house is light, airy, and as cool as water. I used hues of white, blue, charcoal, and black and mixed them with warm, natural wood tones. Every room has visual space to rest the gaze and draw attention to views of the lake.

CHAPTER 14

AUTHENTICITY

{ **au·then·tic** / ə-then'-tik – adj.
that can be believed or accepted; trustworthy; reliable
that is in fact as represented; genuine; real }

Opposite: In my clients' home, which is a former consulate, we had the millwork painted a slightly deeper ivory than the walls to emphasize it ever so slightly and to add a bit of subtle age to the house.

TRUTH, AND OUR RECOGNITION OF THAT TRUTH, is what makes art, in any form, good. A good movie resonates with us because we find truth in its observations and it elicits emotions in us. A photograph of a soldier and his or her family being reunited at the airport might be powerful because there is truth in the emotion in it, because it's honest and authentic.

Authenticity in decorating is about being real, being true to yourself, and being true to the essence of a house. It's about observing surroundings and thoughtfully expressing the style and passions of the people who live there— to convey truths about those people—while never losing sight of the house itself. Architecture, furnishings, a home's surroundings, the land it sits upon, personal style, and the use of quality materials are all integral to creating an authentic home.

To explain what I mean by *authentic* in decorating, I think it's helpful to point out what is not. When I finished college, my first apartment became a design laboratory of sorts (my poor, sweet, patient roommates!), and, without realizing it, I was creating rooms that had themes. Rather than considering our interests or where we lived or what colors we liked, I began with a piece of furniture or an object in each room and literally designed the room around that piece. My aunt gave me a chippy painted blue early-American hutch for the dining room, so I brought in other early-American pieces, painted the walls blue, and paid absolutely no attention to the 1970s architecture of my apartment building or the neighboring rooms in the apartment, which happened to include an olive green living room full of all things Eastern and a terra-cotta–colored kitchen with faux wine-country art. Oh, it was interesting, to say the least. The dining room worked fairly well, but it was completely out of sync with the other, completely contrived rooms, and it made no sense for a garden apartment in Northern Virginia. I'd basically created a series of themed rooms that had no relation to one another, the apartment itself, or to those of us who lived there.

Opposite: In this bedroom in a mountain house, new and antique furnishings mix with a pair of vintage olive green lamps with new black shades, as well as a kitschy collection of vintage paintings of mountain scenes.

Above: This kitchen sits in the addition off the back of a historical house in the city. Our client wanted a hardworking and welcoming kitchen where family and friends alike would feel at home. We incorporated timeless selections such as marble countertops, a classic subway tile backsplash, painted black Windsor stools, copper pots, and antique barrister bookcases in lieu of upper cabinetry to create a space that feels fresh and modern yet appropriate to the age and style of the home.

Furniture, color, art, and all the things that go into a room are our tools for creating atmosphere, and though I was learning how to manipulate style and mood at the time by creating these out-of-place, stage-set-like rooms, I didn't understand that the atmosphere itself needed to be authentic to the house and the other rooms around it in order for the space to truly feel right. Designing a room that fits within the whole is what makes a room, and the entire home, feel authentic. It's possible to move through a house and decorate room by room, but it's vital that we keep the vision of the entire home at the forefront of every design.

To be true to where you live, pay attention to your home's architecture, surroundings, and neighborhood. Take photographs of the exterior of your home and its surroundings to study. Walk around your neighborhood to make sure you understand the attributes of where you live, and take in the flavor. Jot

down notes that describe what you're seeing and feeling. Think about how the vibe around you can mingle with the feeling you want inside your home. Enjoy it. Maybe your personal style is very different from what you're seeing outside, so think about how bringing a little of the exterior's style into your home and juxtaposing it with your own style and meaningful pieces can be interesting and fun and can quite possibly even enrich your own aesthetic.

Bring in elements and materials that call to mind your home's origins. This doesn't mean you need be a purist and worry that every little thing in your home be period-appropriate; it simply means you need to be mindful of your house itself. Architecture is a major component of authenticity. A home full of appropriate architectural elements feels immediately authentic, whereas one completely lacking in architectural details or one with mismatched architecture feels "off" and hollow. If you live in a traditional home but love modern furnishings, it's possible to make the dichotomy work by respecting the house's architecture and playing with it. Keep and/or restore appropriate woodwork and moldings, make sure that hard goods and permanent selections are in materials that could have been original to the home but that have a modern sensibility, and carefully select furnishings that are timeless. If you plan on mixing traditional with modern, make sure you have a few "bridge" pieces that will work well with not only the architecture of the home, but also with both the traditional and modern pieces you plan on incorporating (see Chapter 15, on Juxtaposition). Upholstery is a heavy-lifter when it comes to bridging alternate styles. When upholstery recedes into the background and doesn't make a strong style statement, it allows other pieces and silhouettes to take center stage and play off one another.

Materials and furnishings can also have an air of authenticity about them. We not only see quality, but we recognize it on a tactile level. Quality feels authentic. (Think of the antique dining table with years' worth of dings that just keeps getting better with age, the silky smooth touch of timeworn marble, soft worn velvet, or the sturdy feel to a heavy, solid-brass plumbing fixture. Faux versions of any of these are available—some very well done and others not so much—but when we are physically present in a space, we appreciate the nuance of quality.) I'll never forget walking into my friends Brooke and Steve Giannetti's home for the first time. I was blown away by not only how everything looked, but also how everything felt. The wood on the floor, the faucet in the powder room, the hardware on the doors—it was all so solid and completely authentic. I left with a

Left: In our clients' Colonial house, originally built in the 1940s, we created a fresh and modern space that remained true to the home's historical origins. We worked with Cunningham | Quill Architects to keep the basic envelope of the house itself classic but mixed in modern pieces (a pair of Barcelona chairs) and more basic pieces that work in both traditional and modern spaces (the simple, slipcovered, track-arm sofa and skirted ottomans). The thirteen-star Federal convex mirror calls to mind the house's traditional origins yet brings a playfully modern sensibility to the room when juxtaposed with the abstract artwork above the sofa and the other modern elements.

Above: In my client's apartment in the city, the view is a strong focal point. We selected modern silhouettes for most of the furnishings, which are a mix of new and mid-century pieces, so that they played nicely with the clean-lined architecture of her building and those surrounding it.

Above: The fifteen-foot window seat in our family-room loft.

This spread: This vacation home is surrounded by mountain views and massive oak trees, so I brought in lots of natural, rustic materials that make sense with the surrounding landscape. The stone in the fireplaces throughout the house matches the stone in the wall surrounding the property, and the natural wood tones in the floors, beams, and furnishings are in keeping with the lushly wooded landscape.

bellyful of Italian food and a mini education. This isn't to say that everything in a space needs to be solid and expensive, but by mixing in a few "real" things here and there, an overall feeling of authenticity can be achieved.

In order for a home to tug at *my* heartstrings, I need to feel a connection with nature indoors, which means, the bigger the windows, the better. I like lots of natural light. I'm never happier than when, indoors, I feel as if I'm outside. After realizing how much my whole family loved watching the seasons change and the wildlife outdoors, we added a fifteen-foot-wide window seat in our house to bring in as much of the view as possible and to have a place where we could all fit to look outside (see page 141). The base of the window seat lifts

up to reveal a massive storage bin where we keep luggage, extra blankets, and large toys. It's become the best spot in the house to relax, nap, and read. One of my favorite memories is of a snowy winter night after my husband and I had just put our boys to bed. We snuggled up on the window seat in the dark, and, because of all the snow, it was so bright outside that we could clearly see a family of deer walking around the glen and nestling together under a pine tree for shelter. It was so quiet and peaceful that we ended up falling asleep watching them. We rarely have the time to do that, but having created the window seat gives us the opportunity to slow down and appreciate the land around us when we can. It's completely authentic to something we highly value and love: nature. When people visit, their first comment is always about the view.

CHAPTER 15

JUXTAPOSITION

{ **jux·ta·po·si·tion** / jək-stə-pə-zi'-shən – n.
the fact of two things being seen
or placed close together with contrasting effect }

THE CONCEPT OF JUXTAPOSITION as it relates to a home is relatively simple: Combining opposing elements creates interest. Juxtaposition introduces layers and pleasing tension into a home. An object or element is noticed and better appreciated when it is next to its opposite or some contrasting element. For example, white looks whiter when it's set against black, and a soft, fluffy bath mat feels all the more soft when stepped onto from a hard tile floor.

Juxtaposition isn't always something I go about incorporating on a conscious level; sometimes it's more of an intuitive urge to create more interest in a room. As I've gone back to homes I've decorated or looked at photos of rooms I admire, I can see that it's an important aspect of a well-done space. When we understand our aesthetic and style, it can be challenging to think about including juxtapositions in a room, because we often have the tendency to select things that are very similar to one another and in keeping with our aesthetic. In order to make certain elements stand out, I often include juxtaposing elements that are slightly outside my clients' comfort zones, whether it's a color or something of an alternate style. Often clients have a natural tendency to zero in on those opposing elements and try to remove them from the plan, but if we don't consciously seek out the inclusion of opposites in our homes, they can get boring, so these are the elements I push for the hardest. In the end, my clients are always amazed at how much they like the things they resisted in the beginning. The more we think about juxtapositions and all their possibilities, the more adept we become at creating them, and it almost always results in a more sophisticated type of design. Everything is made stronger when set against its opposite.

Opposite: In this bedroom, the warmth of the vintage burlwood dressers contrasts with the coolness of the polished-steel bed frame. Rough grass cloth sets off all of the glossy surfaces.

Opposite: In an otherwise traditional dining room, modern glass pendant lights contrast with the classic elements, such as the skirted chairs, the bamboo chairs, and the farm table. The chartreuse fabric on the chairs is bright and bold set against the calmer navy walls.

Top, left: In my clients' formal home, simple unlined ivory linen curtains and a giant brown sea sponge contrast with the more sophisticated elements in the room, such as the velvets, silks, and gilded finishes, creating a much more interesting space.

Top, right: In a modern home, antique or primitive pieces can feel like works of art. We placed a pair of antique Chinese wine jugs (one shown here) to contrast with the sleek white envelope of the room.

Left: Recognizing beauty in everyday objects such as this old piece of wood is a good place to start when thinking about juxtaposition. Picture it near lucite or polished nickel.

HABITAT

In the end, it's all about creating balance. Some of the most interesting interior juxtapositions are:

new versus old / shiny versus matte / curvy versus straight / rough versus smooth / soft versus hard / feminine versus masculine / light versus dark / grand versus humble / traditional versus modern / formal versus casual.

Texture is key in making a room interesting to the touch. Even when we aren't actually touching anything in a room, our eyes observe textures, and we have a visceral experience of them. Soft materials appear even softer when next to hard materials.

I believe the old-versus-new juxtaposition is one of the most important. To me, a room filled with only brand-new pieces and objects feels like a store catalog or an ad, and a room filled purely with old things, however beautiful, can quickly feel like a museum or a historical site. Homes get interesting when they are an organic blend of old and new. Every space should have some items with age and patina, whether it's the furniture, finishes, or fabrics. This creates a sense of history and makes the room feel as if it was "collected" with care slowly over time.

Similarly, in a historic home, contemporary furnishings and accessories mixed with older ones make the home feel fresh.

If you don't naturally tend to put unlike elements together, try to push yourself toward it. It might be difficult at first, but it will become easier with time and practice. It's all part of the balancing act of a home. Pretty rooms can—and do—exist without juxtaposition, but truly interesting rooms cannot.

Left: The living room in a historical bluestone in Washington, DC, retains its traditional architectural features, such as the bluestone fireplace and moldings, but surprising modern elements—like the mid-century–inspired Sputnik chandelier and burl wood mirror and table—enliven it.

CHAPTER 16

COMFORT

{
com·fort / kem'-fert – n.
a state of ease and quiet enjoyment;
freedom from pain or worry
}

Opposite: A deep sink-into sofa and pair of chairs sit at opposite ends of this casual, comfortable living room.

ALMOST EVERY SINGLE CLIENT MY FIRM works with requests a "comfortable" home. Everyone's version of "comfortable" is unique, but all versions seem to entail more than merely physical needs. Comfort involves convenience, organization, thoughtful furniture arrangement and lighting selections, the use of products that are both beautiful and functional, and an overall inviting atmosphere. Comfort is about feeling cared for and relaxed. A comfortable home should be designed around the lifestyle of those who live in it.

Think about what's comfortable to you personally, and figure out how you can incorporate it into your home. For example, I love throw blankets. I use them all over my house, and it's not unusual for me to have multiples in each room. I fold them over the backs of sofas or chairs and stash them in baskets. I can enjoy a space without a good throw, but I'm much happier if there's one in the room. I also love deep, sink-into, down-wrapped sofas where I can curl up. Nothing is as cozy as snuggling up on a velvet sofa. I'll often do velvet throw pillows where an entire velvet sofa might not be practical. In the kitchen, I'm most relaxed when I can make a mess on the big island that my family hangs out around as we're preparing meals. In my bathroom, I like to keep piles of fresh white towels to choose from so I can grab one whenever I need it. I also prefer large nightstands or dressers so that when I'm fumbling around for things at night, I don't run out of space and knock things over. Though not always the prettiest choice, I also love ceiling fans above the bed on hot summer nights. All these things make me feel comfortable. For your own home, think about your own needs, wants, and quirks. What will put *you* at ease?

Window treatments and privacy are especially important to consider for comfort, and people often have very strong opinions on them. Do you need privacy at night? Light-filtering needs in the daytime to combat a harsh glare? How do you prefer to sleep at night and wake up best in the morning: with the absolute darkness of blackout shades or with simple, light-filtering shades?

When you get out of bed in the morning, do you prefer for your feet to hit the bare floor, or do you like a soft carpet?

So many factors go into creating a comfortable home. On page 154 are a few universal guidelines I follow in almost every home.

Left: There's something incredibly cozy and comfortable about a pillow-filled window seat.

153

THE COMFORT GUIDELINES

+ Make sure there is a place—a tabletop or horizontal surface of some sort—where you can rest a drink, book, or phone near every seat in the house.

+ In rooms made for relaxation, have a spot for everyone to put his or her feet up, whether it's an ottoman, coffee table, or a sofa to lie down on.

+ Think about the furniture on which you will be spending the most time, and invest in those pieces for better quality and more comfort. If you have children and foresee lots of roughhousing and jumping on the upholstery, remember that, generally, upholstery of a higher quality can take more of a beating than the cheap stuff. If there is to be only one piece in a room that a client is willing to splurge on, I more often than not recommend that it be the sofa.

+ Think about the durability of the materials you select: Fabrics that clean easily or don't show wear and tear, washable slipcovers, table surfaces that don't need coasters, and patterned rugs that hide spills put people at ease. You don't want guests coming into your home and being afraid to touch things.

+ If you plan on hosting long dinners in the dining room, comfortable chairs are a must. An upholstered seat is nice, and a fully upholstered chair is even better. I love slipcovered dining chairs for their practicality. Also, many mid-century dining chairs with ergonomic molded or caned seats are fairly comfortable.

+ Ample storage is also necessary for comfort. If a room is full of clutter, its occupants cannot relax and enjoy themselves. Many activities have specific storage requirements—reading requires attractive storage for books; checking the mail typically requires a fairly central location but one that can be tucked away when not in use; homework often calls for an array of specific supplies; children's toys require storage—so be sure you plan a space that accommodates all a room's functions.

+ In the kitchen, countertop areas of three feet wide or more are most comfortable. Many kitchens have multiple two-foot stretches, but it's better to have fewer unbroken stretches of countertop than lots of small ones so that you can spread out when you're working.

+ Make sure there is a lamp near any seat where reading is planned, be it the bedroom, a living room, or a library.

+ All installed lighting—wall sconces, ceiling fixtures, and recessed lighting—should be on dimmers.

+ Generally, recessed lights are neither "comfortable" nor flattering. Despite the general designer qualm that recessed lighting looks like Swiss cheese on a ceiling, I'm not completely averse to it in areas where it is functionally necessary and where another sort of fixture isn't practical, such as in the kitchen. If you do have to have it, plan the remaining lighting in the room as if there are no recessed lights, with ample table, floor, and wall lamps so that you only need to use the recessed lights for specific tasks.

+ And finally, let go. Ultimately, feeling comfortable comes down to letting ourselves relax and just be in the moment. Loosen up a little, and realize that real homes have a bit of mess at times—usually more than we'd all like—but that's okay. Our houses and everything in them will wear over time, and that's simply part of life. It's more important to focus on actually living than on creating the perfect stage set on which to go about our days. True comfort is a mind-set.

Opposite: An oil painting in shades of green and aqua painted by my client hangs above the sofa in her family room.

CHAPTER 17

LUXURY

{
lux·u·ry / lək′sh(ə-)rē – n.
1. something inessential but conducive to pleasure and comfort
2. something expensive or hard to obtain
3. sumptuous living or surroundings
}

Opposite: Freshly picked wildflowers add a simple bit of luxury to this mountain house bedroom.

LONG ASSOCIATED WITH EXCLUSIVITY AND MONEY, luxury has, I believe, more recently taken on a new meaning. It's no longer only about what can be bought. Luxury is having space and time and organization. It's the simple things that often make one feel truly pampered, not necessarily the expensive ones: crisp, freshly laundered sheets; a hearty, homegrown meal; an unexpected bouquet of flowers; time to sit and read with family. These are the types of luxuries we can fill our lives with on a daily basis if we design our homes thoughtfully. To me, luxury at home is a general ease of life combined with special little "somethings," rather than extravagance. As I plan homes, I try to think about where unexpected luxuries and surprises can be added to make the houses special: shelves for books, a window seat, a place to display treasures, a massive sofa outside, or an outdoor fireplace. For some, luxury could mean an extra sink in the kitchen for washing garden vegetables, or French doors that open to the outside in every room. For others, it's a walk-in closet, a fireplace in the bedroom, a commercial-grade range in the kitchen, a porch swing, a library, a piano in the living room, a soaking tub in the bathroom, a fabric that evokes memories, a kitchen garden, the perfect reading chair, or having a guest bedroom for visitors.

To bring luxury into a house, I take the time to observe and record what the people who will live there really want in their home. What are the owners passionate about? Do they have any collections that would thrill them to display? What excites them? What makes them feel pampered? Is it food? Entertaining? Sports? Crafts? Movies? Nature? Reading? A "man cave" is a form of luxury for many men. It's not necessary for daily life, but it makes them so happy.

Having the space to nurture your passions is a luxury. For my husband, I'm not sure much has ever made him giddier than having enough space for all our books.

The outdoors is one of my favorite places to be, so I adore spaces that blend the indoors with the outdoors. Anything that can be done outside feels like pure luxury to me: an outdoor kitchen, alfresco dining, an outdoor living room, an outdoor shower—I love it all!

Opposite: A glamorous closet for "her."

Above, left: A freshly made bed, one of life's simple luxuries.

Above, right: A bar at the ready in our clients' living room makes entertaining a breeze. A treasured sculpture sits on top of the 1940s piece, and old family photos and keepsakes fill the wall, sparking memories and conversation.

There's luxury in the quality of materials and craftsmanship, which can often be recognized by touch. Think of the hardware on a door that feels strong and solid as opposed to delicate and light; the soft, smooth, cold touch of marble versus plastic; a 100 percent cashmere blanket; a thick terrycloth robe. Whenever possible, try to bring quality into the home, things that will last longer and that you truly appreciate.

There's luxury in uniqueness. Original works of art, handcrafted items, and one-of-a-kind antiques all tell a story and are more interesting than mass-produced pieces.

There's luxury in free time. Many people say that the greatest luxury is time with their loved ones. Think about how you can design a home so precious time isn't wasted on mundane tasks, so that more time can be spent doing what you love. Being organized saves time. Being able to pack for a trip quickly and efficiently because the closet is organized reduces stress. Cleaning up the kitchen is a breeze when there's a place for everything. There is luxury in convenience and in having things close at hand. It all makes life easier.

Opposite: A table set with my grandmother's china in the outdoor covered dining area in the woods in our backyard.

Left: In our home, we enclosed a small, unloved, rocky area just outside our master bedroom doors and created a private little garden patio with an outdoor shower. For me, this is the ultimate luxury.

161

Opposite: My clients had switches installed behind their nightstands for their bedroom lights so they can easily switch off the lights from bed at night. It's one of those little luxuries that makes them, especially the husband, happy.

Above: There is luxury in simplicity and in the calm that results from it.

To get yourself into a luxury mind-set, ask yourself what your dream for each and every space in your home would be. Do you have spaces that are unused? Do you have enough storage? What are your passions? How can you incorporate them in an unexpected way in your home? Do you have room in your backyard or on your balcony to create a special oasis? Do you love watching movies? Can you add a viewing screen and projector anywhere? Do you love to have music on in every room? Can you have a wireless sound system installed? Do you love having fresh-cut flowers all the time? Does your property have a spot for a flower garden? Do you frequently throw big parties? How about an outdoor kitchen or fire pit?

Write it all down, no matter how big or small. Once you have a list, begin to think about how you can actually incorporate these luxuries into your home. Never be afraid to ask for cost quotes. Maybe you can't go after everything at once, but once you've got a wish list, you've taken the first step toward potentially fulfilling it over time.

CHARM

MY MOTHER-IN-LAW, THOUGH SHE WOULD BE THE FIRST to tell you she has not yet fully decorated her house, is a master at creating a charming home. Every time we arrive at my in-laws' house, she has fresh flowers about, beds are made, candles are lit at mealtimes, something yummy is cooking in the kitchen, and the softest, warmest hugs are offered to everyone. Her house may not be decorated exactly as she'd like it to be, but she piles on the charm.

Opposite: Overscale botanical wallpaper— Botanique Spectaculaire by Cowtan & Tout—in a guest bedroom feels at once nostalgic and fresh.

Throughout this book, I've talked about the deliberate planning, the thoughtfulness, and the patience that are required to get everything in a house just the way you want it, but the wonderful thing about charm is that you can create it at almost any stage of decorating. Charm is about graciousness and personal touches that make people feel special, comfortable, or excited. It's not necessarily about the perfectly finished home but rather a person's experience in that home: how it feels, looks, sounds, and even smells. Is it comfortable? Do visitors feel free to relax and let go? Are they inspired by their surroundings? Do aspects of the home cause delight? Charm is all the things that give us that wonderful "homey" feeling and, quite frankly, just make us feel good.

A charming home looks and feels lived-in and loved. It is inviting and gives visitors a sense of who lives there because it feels deeply personal. It results from a willingness to not take oneself too seriously. Charming houses can be large or small, but no matter the size, they feel welcoming and approachable. They can be done in any design style—be it traditional, modern, cottage, etc.— but they feel as if they've been created over time, without a ton of calculation, as if they've come to be almost by way of chance.

Often what feels meaningful or personal to us is something that reminds us of our past. Growing up, I spent a lot of time alone exploring the different houses we lived in, observing everything in them: fabrics, tile, wallpapers, furniture, art, and accessories. Even as a preschooler, I loved looking at beautiful and interesting things. The fabrics and patterns from my past are so ingrained

in my memory that they influence my work today. When I work on designs for my fabric line, I'm amazed by how many of my ideas spring directly from the patterns of my past. It's made me realize that what we put in our homes today affects not only our present, but may also be the backdrop for our future memories and our little ones' memories and their future design sensibilities.

I love watching children's reactions to newly completed spaces. They're incredibly insightful and surprisingly appreciative of interior design. I love it when one of my kids asks to be lifted up to see something closer or tells someone, "Mommy drew that pattern." I'm not sure any of my children will be as sentimental about these things as I am, but I'm betting that a little bit of appreciation for design will rub off on them.

When I come across pieces that remind me of things my two grandmothers had over the years, I often buy them on the spot. Seeing them gives me a feeling that's similar to first waking up from a dream you can't quite remember, but when you finally do, it's oddly satisfying. To this day I like looking through my grandmother's linen closet at her sheet sets, and I still feel an involuntary twinge of excitement when I see the vintage, leafy green, printed futon being pulled down from the garage, because that used to signal that my cousins were coming to visit.

Just as bringing in things that are loved adds charm to a home, so do little inconsistencies and quirks. A room can become so right when something's just a tiny bit off. You don't want to go too far in either direction, though, so a balance of perfection and imperfection is key.

Whether your decorating is where you want it to be or not, you can always bring on the charm. Charm is more than things that can be bought; it's an attitude that entails caring about making everyone who enters your home feel good.

Opposite: This bedroom is humble and personal, mixing old, new, and family pieces in a sea of blue and gray.

Above: My clients, a young couple, save their favorite fortunes in an antique dish passed down through the husband's family.

Above: Cheerful yellow accents on the seats of the mid-century Belgian chairs and on the vintage lamp add charm to this spare dining room. I had the windows, doors, and mullions painted black throughout the house to create tension between light and dark.

Above: I can't help but smile when I see this photograph of a herd of sheep who look to be posing for the camera by Kevin Russ, found on One Kings Lane, hanging in the dining room of my cousin's mountain house. It's so out of left field and cracks everyone up, yet it's still a beautiful photo.

Above: I brought attention to the angles in the ceiling of this top-floor bedroom sitting area by wallpapering them, along with the walls, in a pinstripe. Attic-type rooms like this feel nostalgic when they're papered on both the walls and ceiling.

Above: Me with my grandfather on the sofa in my grandparents' home in Honolulu. I remember always loving the peach, cream, and green chinoiserie floral pattern on the sofa. I am working on a new pattern for my textile line that looks different from this yet captures its essence.

Right: In our foyer, an antique hall tree adds charm to the small space and provides all the functions we need—a mirror for quick checks on the way in or out, a bench for putting on shoes, storage space for stashing, and hooks for hanging.

Opposite: In this mountain house family room, a mid-century-style sofa mixed in with more classic pieces creates a collected vintage vibe. Shelves filled with a jumble of books and mementos serve as a charming backdrop, and wildflowers collected along the mountainside are natural and completely unassuming.

CHAPTER 19

RISK & CONFIDENCE

{
risk / risk – vt.
1. the possibility that something bad or unpleasant will happen
2. to expose to the chance of injury, damage, or loss

con·fi·dence / kän'-fa-dəns – n.
1. the fact of being or feeling certain; assurance
2. belief in one's own abilities
}

Opposite: My client knew she wanted white painted wood floors before she even laid eyes on her house. She grew up in Hawaii and always lived in light, bright houses, which heavily influenced her aesthetic. Stark white simplicity in the kitchen leaves lots of room for bright colors in flower arrangements and table settings. Most homes in the Washington, DC, area have more traditional flooring, and white floors are a trend that go in and out around the country, but my client doesn't care what others are doing, only that she loves it. That's confidence.

WITH A DEFINITION SUCH AS "the possibility that something bad or unpleasant will happen," you're probably wondering if this chapter is worth reading. But, as the saying goes, with great risk comes great reward—and it's just as applicable to decorating as it is to the rest of life.

Decorators and clients take design risks in inspirational homes all the time, but I find that many homeowners are actually a little cautious. What they love in a picture might scare them in real life. But things are more interesting when they challenge us a little. A design risk shouldn't make a client sick with anxiety, but he or she should be slightly nervous, have "Am I really going to do this?" thoughts, and may even be a bit giddy. We all have to accept that it might not turn out okay. If we're not truly excited and are only a trifle anxious about the design choices we're making, I don't think we're pushing ourselves enough. If we do what comes easily without much thought and deliberation, we end up with something nice that works and is pretty but that doesn't excite or entertain us.

What defines risk on a personal level is making a choice that is outside an individual's comfort zone. These comfort zones vary widely. For many of my clients, a little step outside might mean going with art that is scaled unconventionally, throwing an "off" color into an otherwise typical color palette, or mixing in a modern piece of art or furniture in a very traditional home.

When designing for my clients, I usually try to push them just a little bit (or a lot, if they want it) outside their comfort zones. A general rule that can be used to create a great room is that you need to take at *least* one risk. Play with unexpected proportions, wallpaper, color, or art. Oversize light fixtures can cause panic, but once everything is in place, they can end up making the

Above: A view from the mezzanine above of the kitchen in my father's lake house. It's open, casual, and unconventional with easy-to-access cutting boards and bread boards on the walls instead of upper cabinets.

Opposite: When decorating, some of us have an initial fear of ending up with a "busy" room; that is, we are afraid of overdoing it. Many people consider wallpaper a big risk, as it can take over a space completely. To create just the right pattern-to-solid ratio for our clients' guest bedroom (see Chapter 7, on Fabric and Pattern), we used solid-toned bedding and a simple rug and fabrics to calm the oversize botanical pattern of the wallpaper.

room. I find that that's how it typically is with risks: They don't look quite right until everything else is in place. Bold wallpaper in an empty room, a newly painted wall, and a colorful sofa sitting alone waiting for the rest of the furniture to arrive—they all look jarring out of context. It's for this reason that, when installing rooms for clients, we like to do the entire room, or home, at once. We don't want our clients walking into a room before it's finished, because—and I know this from experience—it frightens them. It's often difficult to imagine a half-finished space completed, especially when you're staring at something that jumps out at you, and you cannot imagine it looking good no matter what else happens.

When a project is finished, though, it almost always seems as if there couldn't have been any other choice than to take that risk. The things that had seemed so chancy simply become special aspects of a room. They don't typically seem outlandish or crazy at all to the people who live in the homes, even though they were initially agonized over.

Opposite: Formal traditional architecture is juxtaposed with colorful, sculptural furnishings. New, antique, and vintage mix to create a home that feels as if it was collected over time. Architecture by Franck & Lohsen.

Above: Bold choices, such as the orange Raoul Textiles fabric on the ottoman and the strong use of black and white throughout, imbue this living room with confidence.

Once we begin making risky decisions, we expand our comfort zones—and, as a result, become harder to surprise and more open to still more design risks in the future. It's akin to developing a palate for new foods: The more you try and experience, the more eager you are to taste new things. Eventually, those original adventurous foods seem status quo. It's satisfying to decorate in a way that challenges you to expand your limits, which can be ever-expanding if you let them. That's not to say that design has to be shocking to be good, but it does need to push us a little. Walking that line between conventional and surprising is what challenges and stimulates us. It's all about keeping it meaningful and real while still pushing your limits, even at the risk of something looking "bad and unpleasant."

I often see homes that may be the complete opposite of what I might have done, but I absolutely love them, because I appreciate the strong point of view

Above, left: This guest bedroom is no-frills, with bare floors, simple furnishings, and an antique four-poster bed dressed in crisp white sheets and a wool ticking-stripe blanket. There's a quiet confidence in such a spare, understated space.

Above, right: Our clients' love for stark contrast and pure forms guided our vision for this dining nook off the kitchen. We worked with kitchen designer Lauren Gagnon to create a simple yet dramatic and super-comfortable family dining area. This included squaring off an awkwardly angled wall to accommodate the banquette and cabinetry behind it. The look is clean and modern yet comfortable. The leather banquette will age beautifully over time and is a cozy, practical spot for long meals. There are hidden outlets under the Corian tabletop for laptop use.

they convey, the confidence of the designer, and the beauty in a well-executed vision. Letting go of any sort of worry about what others are doing or where the trends are heading is part of gaining this decorating confidence, which is a fearlessness of sorts. You can be aware of what's in vogue, but don't let that dissuade you from following through with your own vision.

When it comes to designing a home, I believe in fully committing to a stance and running with it. When we have complete confidence in our design vision for a space and in ourselves and our team to execute it, we're able to say yes to design risks, because we're no longer afraid of them. We understand that half measures won't help us achieve our vision, and that to create something truly special, we must have the confidence to go all the way. Go big or go home. Commit.

Once we've gone through the process of defining our aesthetic, developing our style, and determining the mood we want to express, we're able to envision how we want our home to be and to formulate our actual plans for it. We trust in the plans and, ultimately, in ourselves, because we know why we're doing what we're doing.

Following spread: My client is young, bold, thoughtful, sophisticated, and witty, and she has an amazing sense of style and love of fashion. A set of vintage chairs was reupholstered in hot pink suede, showcasing her love of gutsy color. The oversize photograph behind the sideboard is of prehistoric cave paintings in France, which fascinate her. The "No You Shut Up" art on the wall gives visitors a taste of her sense of humor and bluntness. The vintage rug in beige and black keeps an otherwise fresh palette from feeling too new and adds a layer of patina to the space. This room is truly her—in dining room form.

People who decorate confidently don't cater to trends. It doesn't matter what color is in or out when someone is picking hues based on what they like rather than on what others are doing. Sound, reasonable logic lies behind their decorating choices. They might ask for opinions from occupants who will be affected by the design or from people whose style choices they trust, but in general, they don't ask everyone and their mother what they think. While shopping in stores, I've actually seen people ask perfect strangers for their opinions. This doesn't make any sense. They have no idea what these other people's homes look like, or what they know or don't know, yet they are willing to let them decide which set of curtains or pillows to take home. If you ever find yourself wanting to ask a stranger for decorating advice, do this instead: Go home, take a look around you, reassess what you need, and get a stronger hold on your vision. Wait to make decisions until you feel confident in yourself.

Don't ever buy or live with something simply because it "works." Take your time, and trust in yourself. Have a reason behind every decision you make. Relying on both intuition and rationale, decorating is a logical art. You can deduce the right paint color for your walls just as easily as you can figure out a mathematical equation.

When you've finished your homework, educated yourself, and searched your soul, the answers become clear. When you know exactly what you're trying to achieve, everything will fall into place. You can move forward confidently. True confidence isn't empty but backed by knowledge, skill, and reasoning.

Confident decorating has a strong point of view and is based around the idea of decorating for those who will actually live in the home, not for anyone else. If you love something that you don't think others will like, do it anyway. It's your home, not theirs.

Confident spaces don't necessarily translate to a broad audience, but to those they do appeal to, the appreciation is deep and intense.

Decorating doesn't need to be over-the-top or dramatic to be confident. On the contrary, confidence is about executing a clear and unfailing vision, which can be simple or complicated. Sometimes confidence is knowing when to stop.

Confidence is about having the guts to take risks, to make a house feel highly personal, to be who you are and portray that in your home no matter what others are doing. The entire design process is a quest to uncover who you are, what your style is all about, how the architecture of your house and the decorating will converge, and how you want your home to feel so that it best embodies you. Once you've figured it all out and have a plan, all that's left to do is to simply get up the courage to go after it.

PART 3

ROOM-BY-ROOM GUIDE

Every room of a house has its own functions and requirements. In this section, I share my thoughts on each specific room and how I typically approach it when decorating. When beginning a project on any room, I naturally start with a to-do list (see page 45) or checklist, which I've listed in each section for your reference and to help you get a jump-start on projects. You can fill in the to-do lists right on the pages of the field guide, snap a photo of them and print, or copy them onto your own paper or project notebook.

Opposite: Our breakfast room with "moth wing," a fabric of mine that was inspired by our visitors frequenting the butterfly bush just outside the windows.

CHAPTER 20

THE ENTRY

THE FOYER PROVIDES THE FIRST PEEK at what's inside your home, and it sets the tone for the entire house. It should be stylish and incredibly functional and say something about those who live there. Because not many actual items can fit into a foyer without blocking traffic, each and every one should be well thought-out and epitomize your style. The central fixture in the foyer not only needs to be functional, it should also be eye-catching and in keeping with the rest of the home. If possible, include a table lamp or wall sconces for a bit of additional warmth. It feels very cozy to walk into a house at night that's aglow with warm lamplight. Be sure to add a statement-making mirror for passersby to check their appearance on the way in or out the door.

A mudroom, though not often the space guests see first, is often a main point of entry for a home's occupants. If you don't have a mudroom but do have a back door or garage door that will see frequent use, think about adding hooks or a bench to create a mini mudroom. It will help keep clutter off the floor, especially in wet or snowy weather.

Entries, whether a foyer in the front of the house or a mudroom in the back, ensure that shoes, jackets, hats, bags, and other belongings are corralled at the door so they don't get discarded in other rooms. In an entrance it is ideal to have a coat closet, but hooks on the wall can also work well for storing coats, bags, and hats. If you have little ones in the house, be sure to include lower hooks that they can reach. Provide a small surface or tabletop with a tray on it for plunking down sunglasses, keys, and mail. This piece can also make a style statement. If you haven't enough space for an actual piece of furniture, hang a vintage soap dish or another unique shelf on the wall for storing or hanging small items.

Not all foyers or mudrooms have room for seating, but a bench or a chair for putting on and taking off shoes and boots is convenient and welcoming. You'll also need a small bit of hidden storage for gloves and scarves. Baskets, pretty boxes, and even vintage luggage work well for this. If you typically remove your shoes when you enter your home, you'll want a spot to store them, too. All entry floors should to be made of a cleanable, washable material that can handle a fairly large amount of moisture, and any rugs should be able to stand up to a lot of traffic and mess. Wool rugs, washable indoor-outdoor rugs, seagrass, and mats are the best options (see Chapter 6, on Rugs).

Opposite: An orb chandelier in this traditional foyer is the first hint at the interplay of modern and traditional that runs throughout the home.

Walls:

....

Closet or Hooks:

....

Table or Chest:

....

Hidden Storage:

....

Chair or Bench:

....

Lighting:

....

Rug:

....

Mirror:

....

Tray:

....

Art and Accessories:

....

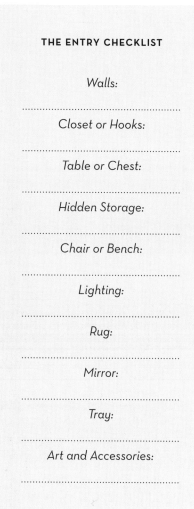

Right: Our clients' antique chest is the ideal drop zone for keys and sunglasses, with extra storage room in the drawers. An onyx lamp on top creates a welcoming glow in the evenings, and the vintage yellow overdyed rug can handle a lot of traffic.

Opposite: A view of the living room from the foyer illustrates how the palette of lemongrass and blues is laced throughout the home.

Left: A newly renovated grand entrance hall feels as if it's always been there thanks to the timeless architecture, salvaged antique marble floor tiles, and antique and vintage furnishings. Architecture by Frank & Lohsen.

Following spread, left: One of a set of four rare blue grisailles in my clients' foyer that was rescued from a manor house in France, just before the French Revolution. It is so striking that little else is needed to make the space feel interesting.

Following spread, right: A narrow mudroom tucked in the back of a family room, although small, packs in function and keeps any mess at bay.

CHAPTER 21

THE POWDER ROOM

Opposite: An existing powder room was revamped with a graphic blue-and-white paper and new lighting and accessories.

THE POWDER ROOM, OFTEN VERY SMALL, is one of the most frequently used public spaces in a home, especially for those who entertain regularly. Generally there isn't much space in the powder room, so everything—the mirror, the hardware, the towels, the art—should be interesting or beautiful. Every choice counts, so make statements wherever possible. Tile and wallpaper are great options for projecting personality onto the walls. Be sure to think about who is using the space. For example, if little ones are in there on a daily basis and splashing is an issue, it's safest to tile halfway up the wall and paper the upper wall and ceiling only. Pedestal sinks or washstands help save space. Small vanities also work well and provide a bit of storage.

The powder room is the perfect place to use a unique or striking faucet. When going with a more typical fixture, I prefer those with an eight-inch spread versus single-hold faucets, because they're more timeless and substantial; but not all pedestals or vanities are set up for eight-inch spreads. The toilet should have as little going on as possible for easy cleaning purposes, and it should be in keeping with the architecture of the house. Towel rods and rings and toilet-paper holders should relate to the hardware throughout the rest of your home. Because such a small amount of hardware is needed in the powder room, it's easy to find interesting vintage pieces. I prefer fairly simple soap dispensers in glass or porcelain bottles. Many beautiful antique and vintage soap dishes are also available. When entertaining, be sure that bars of soap look fresh and new (no one wants to touch a barely-there, well-used nub of soap). Always be sure that powder-room towels are fresh and clean. If the room has a window, opt for treatments that will stay out of the way, such as Roman shades, roller shades, or shutters. Really try to have fun when decorating the powder room. I can't tell you how many conversations at parties are about something interesting, beautiful, or funny in the powder room. Think charm (see Chapter 18, on Charm), and try to inspire delight in your guests.

THE POWDER ROOM CHECKLIST

Walls, Ceiling, and Woodwork:

....

Vanity:

....

Countertop Sink:

....

Faucet:

....

Toilet:

....

Mirror:

....

Lighting:

....

Hardware:

....

Soap Dispenser or Dish:

....

Window Treatment:

....

Towels:

....

Art and Accessories:

....

Right: A marble countertop and oversize backsplash sit atop a vintage dresser.

Opposite: My client's original 1920s bungalow bathroom was given a face-lift with the addition of a simple wooden vanity, lighting, mirror, hardware, and accessories. The old and new elements mix and make sense within the greater context of the house itself.

CHAPTER 22

THE LIVING ROOM

Opposite: A trio of abstract paintings hangs over a low velvet sofa in our clients' living room. A vintage patchwork kilim adds a graphic punch.

Following spread: A pair of unmatched sofas flanks a seamless fireplace. Patinated sheet-metal sculpture/coffee table by Stephane Ducatteau.

LIVING ROOMS CAN AND SHOULD BE TRULY USED and lived in, which is why they should be filled with things that are not only beautiful, but also practical and comfortable. Books, magazines, throw blankets, and meaningful objects in the living room help create a relaxed, personal feel and encourage everyday use. Typically, living rooms are more formal than family rooms and great rooms, and are used as a gathering space for family and friends. Our living room is open to our kitchen, and we use it every day. We keep books and magazines on tiered end tables throughout for convenience, and we love having frequent fires in the fireplace. The lack of a TV encourages conversation, reading, and games.

THE LIVING ROOM CHECKLIST

Sofa / Sofas:

....

Pair of Chairs:

....

The "Odd" Chair:

....

Coffee Table:

....

End Tables:

....

PAIR FLANKING SOFA:

....

TABLE NEAR FIRST CHAIR:

....

TABLE NEAR SECOND CHAIR:

....

TABLE NEAR "ODD" CHAIR:

....

CONSOLE:

....

Ceiling Lighting:

....

Table Lamps:

....

Wall Lights:

....

Floor Lamps:

....

Rug:

....

Window Treatment:

....

Throw Pillows:

....

Throw Blankets:

....

Art and Accessories:

....

Right: A mix of chintz, blue velvet, green silk, tiger-striped rugs, and warm wood tones creates a sophisticated yet energetic vibe in our clients' formal living room. Architecture by Franck & Lohsen.

Above: New built-ins provide architectural character and storage in this historic home. A pair of nineteenth-century paintings in their original gilded frames almost seems to glow against the gray-blue walls.

Opposite: A massive vintage coffee table and extra-deep sofa with down cushions keep this living room relaxed and comfortable. A collection of American historical portraits, including some of the most important Native American leaders throughout history, covers the wall.

CHAPTER 23

THE DINING ROOM

Opposite: The laid-back dining area of my father's family lake house is grounded by a large black slipcovered dining bench. Vintage rattan chairs are pulled up to a custom extra-long trestle table by the Lorimer Workshop. The ceiling was so high that I decided to use a modern arc lamp above the table instead of a traditional chandelier.

DINING ROOMS ARE OFTEN AMONG the most underutilized spaces in a house, but if they are inviting, comfortable, and practical enough, they are much more likely to see use on a regular basis. I like to change things up at home, so we have some meals in the kitchen, some outside, and some in the dining room; varying the location keeps mealtime interesting. Comfortable dining chairs are a must, and, if possible, go with upholstered pieces for long, relaxing dinners. Our dining room chairs are slipcovered so that I don't have to worry about spills on the upholstery, but we also keep a pair of dark gray towels in the room for our (pretty messy) little guys to sit on during dinner so we needn't launder the slipcovers multiple times each week. We use a cowhide rug beneath the table, because no amount of spilled food or drink seems to hurt it. Whenever we eat in the dining room, we light candles and play music to make the meal feel more special.

THE DINING ROOM CHECKLIST

Dining Table:

....

Host Chairs:

....

Side Chairs:

....

Sideboard:

....

Lighting:

....

CHANDELIER:

....

TABLE LAMPS ON
SIDEBOARD OR SCONCES:

....

ACCENT LIGHTING, IF POSSIBLE:

....

Rugs:

....

Window Treatments:

....

Candlesticks:

....

Art and Accessories:

....

Right and opposite: An elegant dining room
in shades of pinky peach and blue is set for
entertaining.

Above: We slipcovered our clients' existing dining room chairs in denim for an easy-to-maintain and casual solution. A pair of dining benches can be pulled up to the expanded table for larger gatherings.

Above: A pair of antique barrister bookcases flanks the doorway in our clients' dining room, unconventionally displaying their china and glassware. A modern chandelier hung low over the traditional burled dining table creates tension and interest.

CHAPTER 24

THE FAMILY ROOM

Opposite: A casual family room with fresh blue-and-green accents.

FAMILY ROOMS SHOULD BE STYLISH, comfortable, and able to stand up to wear and abuse. They should not only look good, but also be simple to maintain with easy-to-care-for materials and plenty of storage to corral all the items that make their way into the space, such as books, magazines, games, and toys. In our house, we have what we call the five-minute rule, meaning that I've made sure to include enough storage in each room that anyone can clean up a mess in five minutes or less. Tiered side tables, cabinets, trays, and baskets are some of my favorite tools for adding attractive storage. Throw blankets are a must in the family room and invite you to curl up and relax. Comfort is paramount in the family room.

Left: The loft in our house serves as a family room/playroom/library. We lined the walls with built-ins to hold our ever-growing book collection. To keep the architecture feeling streamlined and organic, I designed built-ins that consist of drywall columns that hold floating butcher-block shelves in between. Kids' books are on the lower shelves, organized by chapter books, picture books, and board books in the baskets. The book niche above the window seat is just deep enough to house my collection of cheesy horror paperbacks that I've had since I was a teen and refuse to part with. (I've turned them backward so their fluorescent spines don't make my eyes twitch. This works out just fine, as they are rarely read, and I've organized them by author, so it isn't too difficult to find what I need when I crave a blast from the past.) A massive sofa is as wide as a twin bed, and we all snuggle up on it for reading or watching movies.

Following spread: This family room sits in a new addition to a historic home. A traditional brick fireplace with raised hearth was added to impart a sense of age to the space and make it feel a part of the rest of the house.

THE FAMILY ROOM CHECKLIST

Sofa / Sofas:

....

Upholstered Chair / Chairs:

....

The "Odd" Chair:

....

Coffee Table:

....

End Tables:

....

PAIR FLANKING SOFA:

....

TABLE NEAR FIRST CHAIR:

....

TABLE NEAR SECOND CHAIR:

....

TABLE NEAR "ODD" CHAIR:

....

Media Unit:

....

Ceiling Lighting:

....

Table Lamps:

....

Floor Lamps:

....

Window Treatment:

....

Throw Pillows:

....

Throw Blankets:

....

Art and Accessories:

....

THE KITCHEN

WE'VE ALL HEARD THAT THE KITCHEN is the heart of a home. Try as we might to convince our guests to hang out elsewhere, the kitchen is always "where it's at," and there's no use trying to fight it. Nowadays, most of us realize that the kitchen is far more than the room where we prepare our food; it's the place where we'll entertain, cook and eat, work on projects, and bond with our families and friends. Embracing that reality, and taking care with the design of the kitchen, are key to a fully realized home.

So many of my best memories took place in a kitchen, including long talks with my mom, cooking and making huge messes with my dad, bonding with my best friends over midnight snacks as a teenager, and my first date with David in college, when he attempted to cook me a steak for Valentine's Day at his place. So much of *life* happens in the kitchen. Having a personal, functional, bespoke kitchen is one of the best ways to make a home feel good. When I'm working on an entire house and in the process of wrapping my head around how I ultimately want the completed home to feel, I typically start in the kitchen. The style, materials, palette, and overall vibe there will affect the style and feeling of the rest of the house.

Every selection in the kitchen should say something about your design style. Kitchens don't provide many opportunities for soft goods, so it's important to make thoughtful choices in plumbing fixtures, lighting, and cabinet hardware. For a relaxed and collected-feeling kitchen, mix metals. A kitchen can feel cold and sterile when each and every finish matches, so have fun with the hardware.

I often design an island to look like a stand-alone piece of furniture and have it done in a different finish and style from the perimeter cabinetry. I often select a different countertop for it, as well. I prefer classic or commercial-looking appliances with clean lines; straight lines are more timeless than space-age curves. Stainless steel is great, but so are other colors and options, such as black or white.

THE KITCHEN CHECKLIST

Cabinetry:

....

Island:

....

Countertops:

....

Backsplash:

....

Flooring:

....

Faucet:

....

Sink:

....

Shelving:

....

Refrigerator:

....

Range:

....

Range Hood:

....

Oven:

....

Microwave:

....

Dishwasher:

....

Hardware:

....

Counter / Island Stools:

....

Lighting:

....

Window Treatments:

....

Art and Accessories:

....

This spread and previous spread: This Belgian-inspired kitchen's floor plan was reworked to allow better flow and focal points. Glazed perimeter cabinets are mixed with a white center island full of practical drawers. Given the copious storage under the counters and in the pantry, upper cabinets weren't necessary. A long shelf above the sink wall holds potted topiaries and ironstone. A mix of warm wood and leather creates a simple yet sculptural dining area.

When designing a kitchen from scratch, I like to center the range or cooktop on one wall and center the sink on another wall, preferably in front of a window. Another option is to set the sink in the island, but it's important that homeowners then understand that, with the mess often associated with washing dishes, a clutter of dirty plates or a pile of clean ones waiting to be dried can prove inconvenient on the center workstation.

While functional, the range hood also offers an opportunity to make a design statement. A large protruding hood in any kitchen instantly becomes a focal point, so take great care to ensure that its style works with your overall vision for the room. One of the things I try to avoid is the arrangement of a microwave oven with an exhaust fan below it over the range. While this setup

is completely functional for a lot of people (I've had it myself in the past), it sacrifices a focal point and changes the room's vibe. I prefer to suspend the microwave under a counter, if possible, or in the upper cabinetry if clients don't want to bend down to it. If a range hood isn't an option for some reason, consider a downdraft cooktop.

In general, although a few cabinets are necessary in a kitchen for larger appliances, I prefer drawers instead of doors whenever possible. They're a bit more accessible than cabinets, and I love that kids can reach things inside and, thus, be more self-sufficient in the kitchen. Drawers can be fitted with racks so that plates and glasses can be stored beneath a counter if desired. I also love open shelving for its airy look and its ability to display things I want

This spread: This mountain-house kitchen, originally very dark and clad in 1970s wallpaper, was completely reconfigured. We added a central window, with sink beneath it, and moved the range to its own wall to create two separate focal points, one on each of the main working walls. Honed absolute black granite countertops with a sixteen-inch-high backsplash are utilitarian and hardworking. An oiled-butcher-block-topped island is warm and practical. An iron pot rack hangs above the range, displaying a small collection of cookware, from cast-iron skillets to a treasured family polenta pot. A stone fireplace at the opposite end of the kitchen adds to the rustic, cozy vibe of the space.

to see or use on a daily basis, such as dishes, cake stands, glasses, and pitchers. Shelving makes a kitchen incredibly accessible; pulling dishes out and putting them away is quicker and easier when you needn't constantly open and close cabinet doors. We entertain frequently, and having open shelving in our kitchen allows guests to truly make themselves at home.

Although I have general preferences and follow certain guidelines in kitchens, I try to approach the design of every kitchen from a blank slate, shaking off as many preconceived notions as I can. One of these preconceived ideas is the usefulness of upper cabinetry. It has become a staple of American kitchens, but it isn't always necessary or functional. I use it only when it makes sense with the architecture, when there is not enough closed storage in the lower cabinetry, or when a client requests it.

I'm neither a believer nor a nonbeliever in the "work triangle" (from refrigerator to sink to stove) in a kitchen; rather, I prefer to think logically through each kitchen as its very own space that needs to be tailored to those who live in the home. I will often separate the refrigerator and microwave a bit from the rest of the fixtures, because I find that space helps when there

are multiple people in the kitchen. I did this in designing my own kitchen; because of space restrictions and because I wanted a larger sink wall, I took the plunge and moved my refrigerator clear across the room from the sink. At first I thought the idea was crazy, and I wasn't quite comfortable with it, but after I walked the length of my kitchen a few times, imagining I was carrying something from the refrigerator to the sink, I realized that I would manage just fine. I had the microwave set into the base cabinetry beside the refrigerator for convenient meal reheating. Now, with the refrigerator—and the constant opening, closing, and water-glass filling that goes on around it— out of my way, I love the setup. It's become its own little station in the kitchen where someone can be doing salad prep while someone else works at the stove or island, and no one gets in anyone else's way. When doing these separated cooling/cooking stations, I often have shelves for glasses and cookbooks installed in the sometimes-awkward space beside the refrigerator.

Previous spread: Whenever possible, I like to center the range on a wall, with a hood above it, flanked by cabinetry, shelving, or artwork to create a strong, symmetrical focal point. In a hard-working kitchen in the new addition of a beautiful historical home, we blended old and new for a fresh collected look. A pair of unexpected antique barrister bookcases flanking the simple plaster range hood adds personality and a sense of history to the space. Metals are mixed throughout for a collected feel. Windsor stools at the island and a skirted sink are nostalgic touches.

This spread: A mix of materials and finishes for the countertops (soapstone on the island, white Caesarstone on the perimeter countertops), the metals (stainless steel, bronze, and brass), and walnut stain and navy blue paint come together in this simple yet functional kitchen. A small coffee and wine bar is both practical and luxurious. A washable vinyl bench in the dining area mixes with modern Windsor chairs creating an interplay of old and new.

Above and opposite, left: A pair of custom iron baker's racks flanks the range and holds everyday dishes, glassware, and serving pieces. Most food prep happens at the large island, and parties naturally seem to take place around it. Floating butcher-block shelves in the nook next to the refrigerator hold glasses, vases, cookbooks, ice buckets, and other kitchen items.

Opposite, right: For sinks in front of windows, I like to have lights hung just above the window. Not only is this practical for washing dishes at night, but it also accentuates the window, much the way a window treatment in another room might.

Following spread: In my father's lake house kitchen, the original upper cabinetry closed in the room and made it feel much smaller, blocked it off from the great room, and called attention to its awkward angles. When the new kitchen was being built, I decided to forgo upper cabinetry altogether to keep the space as open and airy as possible. Dinnerware and glassware is stored in drawers that have been fitted with organizers to keep them from sliding around when the drawers are opened and closed. An awkward ceiling transition made having a range hood impossible, so I selected a range with a retractable downdraft.

This spread: In this galley kitchen, upper cabinetry was employed to maximize storage space and a large window was added, closing off an exterior door and a second dining-room entrance to create still more storage and allow the sink wall to become a focal point. A tumbled-marble backsplash adds a bit of patina to the new space, and cork floors laid in a harlequin pattern are soft underfoot and create energy and pattern in the kitchen. The Bertazzoni range is a favorite of our clients, who love to cook and host intimate dinners. They eat most meals at the comfortable upholstered banquette, which feels like a giant sofa pulled up to the table.

This spread: A combination of cabinetry and open shelving gives this kitchen a good amount of both open and closed storage. Everyday plates, bowls, glasses, and mixing bowls are displayed on the shelving, while less-attractive items are stored behind closed cabinet doors. Soapstone countertops sit atop both gray perimeter cabinetry and the white island cabinetry. A large washable navy slipcovered banquette faces woven rush chairs in the dining area. A collection of antique botanicals adds to the natural feel of the space.

CHAPTER 26

THE BEDROOM

Opposite: Natural textural elements such as the rattan bed, burlap stools, and bamboo shades combine well with traditionally elegant furnishings and fabrics. Newly added painted wood paneling on the walls lends a sense of permanence to the room.

BEDROOMS, OUR PERSONAL RETREATS, should put us instantly at ease. These spaces should also make sense with the rest of the home, but a little deviation from the color palette often works well. I prefer to keep my bedroom as simple, neutral, and uncluttered as possible, because so much of the house seems to end up in there, and it's all quite colorful: my kids' toys, laundry, piles of books, water glasses, shopping receipts, my clothes, and random everything else. If you want your bedroom to feel exciting, but you also want to relax at night, create a focal point out of your bed wall, and keep all else relatively simple. I have an Alice-in-Wonderland–like gallery wall of botanicals above my bed that I enjoy when I'm up and about, but I don't see it when I'm lying in bed. (See page 76.) I love having nothing too busy to look at while I'm trying to fall asleep but something that excites me during the day.

Keep nightstands relatively clear of decorative objects—with the exception of a vase of flowers or greenery—so there's room for the essentials: lamp, phone or clock, book, water glass, eyeglasses. I also keep a little tray on one side of the bed to corral my hair bands and lip balm.

Bedding preferences are extremely personal. I often do layered beds that will change a bit seasonally depending upon temperature. I won't get deeply into sheets and thread counts here, but I suggest determining whether you prefer a cool sheet or a warm one before starting your hunt for the perfect linens. You can tell just by rubbing your hand over a sheet if it feels warm or cold. Quality sheets, made from cottons with longer fibers, will stay smooth (not pill) longer.

THE BEDROOM CHECKLIST

Bed:

....

Dresser:

....

Nightstands:

....

Chair:

....

Lighting:

....

BEDSIDE LIGHTS:

....

ADDITIONAL LAMP:

....

CENTRAL LIGHT OR CEILING FAN:

....

Rug:

....

Sheets:

....

Duvet Cover:

....

Duvet Insert:

....

Blanket or Quilt:

....

Bedskirt:

....

Art and Accessories:

....

Above: In our lake house bedroom I flanked a modern upholstered bed with a pair of warm wooden mid-century nightstands. Vintage nightstands are fairly easy to come by and I often use them to bring patina to a bedroom when the bed is new.

Opposite: New and vintage elements mix in a glamorous bedroom swathed in gray grasscloth. Architecture by Franck & Lohsen.

Following spread, left: A 1930s Kars rug, a vintage leather bench, and an old spindle table and lamps mixed with new hand-block-printed bedding by Les Indiennes come together for a collected feel.

Following spread, right: A small settee and antique trunk at the foot of the bed provides a spot to sit in the bedroom.

CHILDREN'S ROOMS

Above: With four kids sharing the space, this lake house bunk room needed as much storage as possible, so we added built-in bunk beds with large drawers beneath for clothing, in addition to a small closet and a dresser. Hooks on the wall help keep random towels, clothing, and bags off the floor.

Kids' rooms often need to pack in even more function than adults' rooms do, because they're often the children's only personal space in the house. Little ones need storage for all their things—books, toys, trophies, and electronics—and often a small workstation. Kids' rooms needn't have themes in order for their occupants to love them; children just need to feel that you took into account their preferences (say, their favorite colors) and to have a place that feels like their own. My boys love all things mainstream—Transformers, trucks, cars, pirates, Batman, and LEGOS—and although their toy bins are full of these items, their bedroom decor isn't. It's similar to the rest of the house in style, although their artwork is a bit more whimsical (they make up stories about it), and the walls are painted one of their favorite colors, blue.

Above: The kids' room at my cousin's mountain house is fairly utilitarian and spare. It has a wall of beds in mismatched wool blankets, papier-mâché animal heads, and homemade headboards, and the kids absolutely love it. They all carve out a little bit of personal space for themselves during their visits. I love peeking in at them at bedtime as they chat themselves to sleep. One of the best things I witnessed was six-year-old Addison saying, "This feels like an orphanage!" and proceeding to sing "It's a Hard-Knock Life."

Right: A pair of cheerful turquoise twin beds in our clients' daughter's bedroom allows her to have sleepovers with her little sister, whose room is down the hall.

GUEST ROOMS

For guest bedrooms, general bedroom guidelines apply, but you can add a few extras to make guests feel at home. Here's my short list:

Water carafe or bottled water

*Clean towels and
a fresh bar of soap*

Extra blankets

Fresh flowers or greenery

Scented candle

Magazines or books

Luggage rack

*Important items and info
(Wi-Fi password, house keys,
train passes and schedule)*

RECIPE FOR THE PERFECT BED

+ *quality mattress*
+ *mattress cover*
+ *your ideal sheets*
+ *duvet cover over down
  or down-alternative insert*
+ *blanket, coverlet, or quilt*
+ *a reasonable amount of pillows
  (Don't go too pillow crazy!)*

Right: A lively mix of patterns by John Robshaw and Lauren Liess Textiles feels fresh and energetic in a client's small guest bedroom.

Opposite: An antique horsebit hangs between a collection of silhouettes in this guest bedroom.

CHAPTER 27

THE BATHROOM

Opposite: Shiplap walls add texture and character to a brand-new bathroom. Soaking tubs are not only incredibly relaxing, but they also add a sculptural element to a space. I often have square tiles laid in a subway pattern as seen in the spa blue tiles for added subtle interest.

BATHROOMS NEED TO BE PRACTICAL AND FUNCTIONAL, but they should be beautiful, too. Select timeless materials that are in keeping with your style and the home's architecture. Stay away from things for the sole reason that they're in style, don't fear things that are supposedly out of style, and choose colors and materials because you love them. As in the powder room, select plumbing and lighting fixtures that feel appropriate with the rest of the house. If more than one person will be using the bathroom and there is enough space, choose a vanity with multiple sinks or use two vanities. Consider topping an old dresser with a new countertop and repurposing it as a bathroom vanity. Use eight-inch-spread faucets or wall-mounted faucets for a statement and for easy cleaning.

Keep bathroom art and accessories to a minimum. Include a bit of art on the walls so that the room doesn't feel sterile, and consider fresh towels, a rug, a basket for supplies, soap, and a vase of flowers. Accessories should be practical and useful. If you plan on lighting candles in the bathroom, have a candle or two, but don't bring in pillar candles that you don't plan to light as decor. It's great if you fill baskets with useful things, such as towels, washcloths, toilet paper, and soap, but baskets holding decorative objects and pretty things you'll never use will simply take up space and collect dust.

THE BATHROOM CHECKLIST

Vanity:

....

Countertop:

....

Sink:

....

Faucet:

....

Toilet:

....

Mirror:

....

Towel Rods or Hooks:

....

Toilet-Paper Holder:

....

Cabinets / Storage Space:

....

Lighting:

....

VANITY LIGHTING:

....

OVERHEAD:

....

Towels:

....

Soap Dish or Dispenser:

....

Art and Accessories:

....

Above: A simple textural bathroom in a mountain home feels quiet and relaxing.

Opposite: One of a pair of his-and-hers floating vanities in a master bath is shown here with vintage-style hex floors. White glass lamps beside the mirrors provide face-flattering light and flush mount square rain shower heads lend a spa-like feel.

Right and opposite:
Symmetry reigns in
our family's lake house
bathroom complete
with double rain shower
heads in polished nickel
and a shower flanked by
metal cabinets filled with
bath supplies. I wanted
us to feel as if we're in
a completely different
setting when we visit the
lake, so I brought in colors
and elements that call
to mind the water and
shore, such as the shiplap
walls and the modern
gray pebble resin floors.
We used an island with a
two-sided mirror and sinks
in lieu of the traditional
vanity because it allowed
for better flow.

CHAPTER 28

THE HOME OFFICE/STUDY

Opposite: An oversize vintage pendant lamp hangs above a project table in a client's home office.

HOME OFFICES, STUDIES, OR LIBRARIES can be separate rooms or small areas carved out of larger spaces. Often, two functions are combined in one room with the use of bookshelves, comfortable seating, and work space. A home office, if organized carefully, helps the entire home function better. Everyone has a preferred method of working, so figure out yours before deciding what type of floor plan and furniture you'll need. I like to work on a large table and spread out a huge mess of papers, or I'll curl up on a sofa with my laptop. The entire family uses our home office, so we need lots of shelving and cabinetry to corral all our not-so-pretty things.

Home offices should be done in a similar style as the rest of the house. Make sure there is enough storage so that the room feels tidy, especially if your home office does double duty as a guest bedroom or any other type of space. Use closets, and try to hide electronics cords behind pieces of furniture, or purchase cord-control systems to keep things neat.

A private library can be a place to relax, think, and disappear in for a while. Home libraries should have comfortable seating for extended lounging and ample task lighting for reading. I have wanted a dedicated library since I was a kid. While not all of us can have an actual library, most of us do have space somewhere in our homes for bookshelves. Our loft, which is really a family room, also functions as a library, because we lined the walls with bookshelves. If you want a library badly enough, try to find a place for it, no matter how small your house is. Consider adding bookshelves in a random hall or stairway to create a mini library. Or line a living room with shallow bookshelves. Bookshelves can function just like walls, and you can place pieces of furniture in front of them if needed, so take a second look if you don't think you have the space for them.

THE HOME OFFICE/STUDY CHECKLIST

Desk / Table:
....

Desk Chair:
....

Reading chair:
....

Side Table:
....

File Cabinets:
....

Storage:
....

Lighting:
....

DESK LIGHT:
....

OVERHEAD LIGHT:
....

ADDITIONAL LAMP / LAMPS:
....

Cord Control:
....

Charging Station:
....

Rug:
....

Window Treatment:
....

Art and Accessories:
....

Above: My client grew up in Hawaii, and these roots heavily influence her personal style. For the interior of her Washington, DC, home, which has very traditional architecture, we subtly wove in lots of bold, tropical patterns and colors, as well as a sense of the ocean.

Above: In my client's historic bungalow, we turned a first-floor bedroom off the living room into a library. At ten feet high, the entire space was painted in a saturated blue, and a rolling ladder was added to allow her to reach books on high shelves. A small antique table-turned-desk sits in a corner with a quirky Schoolhouse Electric lamp. My client reads in the window seat and loves taking naps there. Soft linens and a faded antique rug lend patina to the room. The shelves have hidden wheels, and a secret door to the bathroom hides behind them. Guests can't help but smile when they visit this beautiful, eccentric library.

Following spread, left: A large worktable in our home office functions not only as a place for me to spread out projects upon, but also as a crafts and drawing table for our kids.

Following spread, right: Seamless cabinetry in this home office hides away all office components, and its sleek white contrasts with the wood tones of the table and floor. The custom central worktable we designed and had built by the Lorimer Workshop is equipped with electrical outlets that make it easy for our clients and their children to charge their laptops and phones.

CHAPTER 29

THE HALLWAY

Opposite: An upstairs hallway serves as an unexpected mini library. A vintage leather chair provides a comfortable reading spot. Architecture by Cunningham | Quill Architects.

WHEN I WAS A KID, HALLWAYS WERE AMONG my favorite places in my grandparents' house, where I grew up. I loved the patterned paper in the upstairs hall and the massive wall of ancestral portraits. My grandmother has always taken great care in every space in her home, and she has never neglected the corridors—where, among other things and to everyone's dismay, I did my cartwheels. Hallways are often a home's forgotten spaces, but a well-designed one makes a house feel more thoughtful and special and can even become one of its most charming spots. Hallways can serve as galleries, displaying interesting pieces of art or photographs. Architectural details, color and texture on the walls, sconces, and mirrors can enliven potentially bland hallways. Never think of a corridor as simply a "pass-through," but use it as a creative opportunity to add function and interest to the home.

THE HALLWAY CHECKLIST

Runner:

....

Bookcases:

....

Bench:

....

Lighting

....

Art and Accessories:

....

Right: A vintage figure study hangs above a newly upholstered family piece in a hallway corner. Architecture by Cunningham | Quill Architects.

Opposite: Architects Franck & Lohsen designed an incredible spiral staircase that spans three floors in our clients' home. A three-stair light fixture by a good friend of mine, lighting designer Rick Singleton, is the "jewelry" for the space.

CHAPTER 30

THE OUTDOOR ROOM

Opposite: During the warmer months, the front porch of my client's historic bungalow serves as another room of the house.

OUTDOOR SPACES SHOULD BE AS WELL THOUGHT-OUT as interior ones. Just as bringing the outside in is often a goal in decorating, bringing the indoors out makes outdoor spaces much more interesting. My family jokes that it's ridiculous that we spent so much time and effort decorating our home's interior, when we spend pretty much every minute possible outside.

We can all extend the time we spend in the fresh air if we create beautiful and practical outdoor dining and living areas. It doesn't take much space to carve out something special. Even a small bistro table and chairs on a balcony provide a spot to get some sunlight and have a drink or a meal. Think about what you have available and how you can use it, and make every inch count.

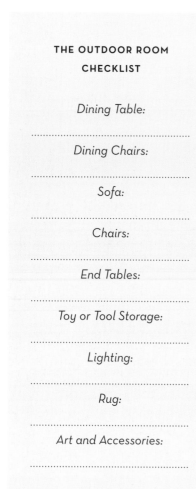

THE OUTDOOR ROOM CHECKLIST

Dining Table:

....

Dining Chairs:

....

Sofa:

....

Chairs:

....

End Tables:

....

Toy or Tool Storage:

....

Lighting:

....

Rug:

....

Art and Accessories:

....

Right: My husband and I converted an old dog pen in our backyard into a "cabana in the woods."

Opposite: A pair of wicker sofas, a rug, and a roughhewn coffee table elevate a simple stone barn.

A FINAL WORD: THERE'S NO SUCH THING AS A DESIGN EMERGENCY

Opposite: Among other things, wild oak leaf hydrangea grows all over the mountain where my cousin's house sits. One of my favorite pastimes is taking the kids for walks to collect wildflowers for every room of the house.

Below: Our vegetable garden is an extension of our house. After coming home from work, I often unwind by picking vegetables and watching the kids play in the yard or sharing a glass of wine with David in the Adirondack chairs. A kitchen garden was something we never really knew we were missing until we had it, yet it has truly changed the way we live. I've even come to think of food differently—tasting it and appreciating it more and becoming more creative with it.

When I first got started in this business of decorating, I heard the saying somewhere, "There's no such thing as a design emergency." Throughout the years I've held that notion close—even when it didn't feel true—in order to keep perspective. I know just as well as anyone else does that design projects can be crazy and busy and stressful, but we should remember that we are truly fortunate to face undertaking decorating of any sort. Most people in the world do not have this luxury; many have no homes at all. So enjoy the process, and try not to wish or worry it away. It's simply about thinking things through, making each decision as carefully as you can, and, in the end, finding the confidence to let go and trust yourself.

Just the way that I stumbled across that first field guide so many years ago, and it gave me a new appreciation for nature, I hope you've enjoyed your stumble across this guide and that it has opened your mind to new ways of living in and loving your home.

RESOURCES

My go-to shops and companies.

BEDDING

JOHN ROBSHAW
johnrobshaw.com

LES INDIENNES
lesindiennes.com

PEACOCK ALLEY
peacockalley.com

PINE CONE HILL
pineconehill.annieselke.com

BOUTIQUES

AND BEIGE
andbeige.com

BROWN
shopbybrown.com

GIANNETTI HOME
giannettiarchitects.com

HOLLYWOOD AT HOME
hollywoodathome.com

HUDSON
hudsonboston.com

JOHN ROSSELLI & ASSOCIATES
johnrosselli.com

KEVIN STONE ANTIQUES &
INTERIORS
kevinstoneantiques.com

OLD LUCKETTS STORE
luckettstore.com

PEAR TREE COTTAGE
thepeartreecottage.com

MECOX GARDENS
mecoxgardens.com

RIVERS SPENCER INTERIORS
riversspencer.com

SCENTIMENTAL GARDENS
scentimentalgardens.com

SOUTH OF MARKET
southofmarket.biz

SPURGEON-LEWIS ANTIQUES
spurgeonlewis.com

TONE ON TONE ANTIQUES
tone-on-tone.com

FURNITURE

HICKORY CHAIR
hickorychair.com

LEE INDUSTRIES
leeindustries.com

THE LORIMER WORKSHOP
lorimerworkshop.com

PALECEK
palecek.com

TAYLOR SCOTT COLLECTION
taylorscottcollection.com

VANGUARD FURNITURE
vanguardfurniture.com

VERELLEN
verellen.biz

FABRICS & WALLPAPER

BLACK & SPIRO
shop.blackandspiro.com.au

COLE & SON
cole-and-son.com

COWTAN & TOUT
cowtan.com

DE GOURNAY
degournay.com

MICHAEL S SMITH INC.
michaelsmithinc.com

JOHN ROSSELLI & ASSOCIATES
johnrosselli.com

KATHRYN M. IRELAND
TEXTILES & DESIGN
kathrynireland.com

KATIE RIDDER
katieridder.com

KRAVET
kravet.com

LAUREN LIESS TEXTILES
laurenliess.com

LES INDIENNES
lesindiennes.com

LISA FINE TEXTILES
lisafinetextiles.com

PAUL MONTGOMERY STUDIO
paulmontgomery.com

PETER DUNHAM TEXTILES
peterdunhamtextiles.com

PHILLIP JEFFRIES LTD.
phillipjeffries.com

RAOUL TEXTILES
raoultextiles.com

ROBERT ALLEN
robertallendesign.com

SCHUMACHER
fschumacher.com

THIBAUT
thibautdesign.com

TRACI ZELLER DESIGNS
tracizeller.com

LIGHTING

ARTERTIORS HOME
arteriorshome.com

BARN LIGHT ELECTRIC
barnlightelectric.com

CIRCA LIGHTING
circalighting.com

MADE GOODS
madegoods.com

OLY STUDIO
olystudio.com

SCHOOLHOUSE ELECTRIC
& SUPPLY CO.
schoolhouseelectric.com

STRAY DOG DESIGNS
straydogdesigns.com

VISUAL COMFORT & CO.
visualcomfort.com

HARDWARE

REJUVENATION
rejuvenation.com

RESTORATION HARDWARE
restorationhardware.com

ROCKY MOUNTAIN HARDWARE
rockymountainhardware.com

NATIONAL STORES

ANTHROPOLOGIE
anthropologie.com

CRATE & BARREL
crateandbarrel.com

DESIGN WITHIN REACH
dwr.com

POTTERY BARN
potterybarn.com

REJUVENATION
rejuvenation.com

RESTORATION HARDWARE
restorationhardware.com

ROOM & BOARD
roomandboard.com

TARGET
target.com

WEST ELM
westelm.com

WILLIAMS-SONOMA HOME
williams-sonoma.com

WISTERIA
wisteria.com

PLUMBING

BRIZO
brizo.com

CALIFORNIA FAUCETS
calfaucets.com

KOHLER
kohler.com

PERIOD BATH SUPPLY COMPANY
periodbath.com

WATERMARK
watermark-designs.com

WATERWORKS
waterworks.com

RUGS

DASH & ALBERT
dashandalbert.com

JAIPUR
jaipurrugs.com

LANDRY & ARCARI
landryandarcari.com

SAFAVIEH HOME FURNISHINGS
safaviehhome.com

TILE

ANN SACKS
annsacks.com

ARTISTIC TILE
artistictile.com

DALTILE
daltile.com

PRATT & LARSON CERAMICS
prattandlarson.com

SUBWAY CERAMICS
subwayceramics.com

WALKER ZANGER
walkerzanger.com

ONLINE

1STDIBS
1stdibs.com

CHAIRISH
chairish.com

DERING HALL
deringhall.com

EBAY
ebay.com

ETSY
etsy.com

ONE KINGS LANE
onekingslane.com

"FILTERS" WORK SHEET

Use this work sheet as a guide to help create a language for your project that will aid you in making design decisions that stay true to your vision.

FILTER	DESCRIPTION	FOR EXAMPLE
AESTHETIC	List the set of principles that guides you in your creative decisions. For example, "_____ is good," "I want _____," or "I appreciate _____."	1. I have a strong appreciation for nature and want it to be woven throughout my life and my home. 2. There is a mix of styles both old and new. 3. I always want the sensation of having breathing room. 4. A sense of timelessness is paramount to me.
STYLE	Style is how your aesthetic will actually look or appear when put into action. Describe your personal style with adjectives.	Natural, eclectic mix of styles, both old and new, overall impression of breathing room, modern yet timeless
HOUSE	Describe your home's architecture and style.	Rustic, airy, open, '70s, modern, timeless
FEEL	Describe how you want to feel at home.	Relaxed, happy, creative, and free
MOOD	Describe the desired mood of your home.	Light and airy, organized, fun, relaxed and natural
COLOR PALETTE	Describe your general color palette.	Neutrals—whites and warm ivories mixed with black and camel tones with small accents of warm golds, greens, and mustards throughout
PROJECT LANGUAGE	Your project "language" is what results from all of this combined information. List the descriptive phrases that apply to your specific project and use the verbiage as a litmus test or filter throughout the design process. Each and every selection of your project should fit through this "filter."	A warm vintage rustic modern mix of collected styles, and timeless, with a strong connection to nature, and an overall impression of space and breathing room. A casual, relaxed vibe is key and the home should make life easier by being organized and conducive to creative endeavors and fun.
FINAL FILTER	Always ask yourself, "Is X in keeping with my overall vision?"	"Is this rug right with my overall vision?" "Is it relaxed enough?" "Is it too serious?" "Are the colors in keeping with my palette?" "Is it too busy?" and so on.

INDEX